Seductive Detective

(a play)

Seductive Detective

(a play)

By
Abubakar Othman

malthouse
Malthouse Press Limited
Lagos, Benin, Ibadan, Jos, Port-Harcourt, Zaria

© Abubakar Othman 2020
First Published 2020
ISBN 978-978-58298-0-8

Published in Nigeria by

Malthouse Press Limited
43 Onitana Street, Off Stadium Hotel Road,
Off Western Avenue, Lagos Mainland
E-mail: malthouselagos@gmail.com
Facebook:@malthouselagos
Twitter:@malthouselagos
Istagram:@malthouselagos
Tel: 0802 600 3203

Distributors:
African Books Collective Ltd, Oxford, UK
Email: abc@africanbookscollective.com
Website: http://www.africanbookscollective.com

The writer writes a play, the actors interpret another, the public sees still another, the critics judge a fourth which is completely, personally, theirs.

-Eugene Ionesco

Characters in Order of Appearance

Class chairman
Male student I
Female student I   Students in Phonetics class
Male student II
Female student II
Zakinnatu Joji

Dr. Kabiru Faruk   Phonetics Lecturer
Dr. Kimaram Tiwe   Poetry Lecturer

Bukar Kaka
Ladi Lamba
Rose Loshin
Sani Mohammed   Students in Poetry class
Mary Shamkong
Pink Lady

Mrs. Lami Kabiru   Wife to Dr. Kabiru Faruk

Agnes James
Yusuf Yakong
Chuckude Igwe
Lamila Saidu

Roommate I
Roommate II   Zakinnatu's room-mates

Student leader   PRO
Speaker of parliament
Professor Wawa Vice Chancellor
Director senate
Committee chairman
Bursar
Professor Amina Garba
Registrar
Professor Hamaseyo Jauro
Panel's secretary
Panel's chairman
Professor Danladi Usman
Mrs. Rabi Mairubo
ASUU Chairman
Dr. Dalla Dalla
Dr. Madu Balami
Mr. Haruna Dauda
Barr. Yusuf Musa
ASUU Secretary
Professor Tembo Mokalkolire
Dr. Laraba Usman
Dr. Mairama Dogo
Director Operations

Movement One

In an imaginary University in Northern Nigeria. It's early in the morning. Students are seen in a lecture hall eagerly waiting for their course lecturer to arrive. A student walks in languidly, exhibiting a sure sign of hangover of sleep. Another student already seated, abruptly gives a loud yawn followed by a strenuous stretching of the hands and cringing of the neck, also signs of hunger or hangover. Others are just merry, chatting among themselves. The atmosphere is generally congenial, suitable for an early Monday morning lecture. Then comes the anti-climax. The class chairman enters boisterously with a message for his fellow students:

CLASS CHAIRMAN: Colleagues, Comrades, Course Mates! Lend me your ears. I have come with a message from our course lecturer, DR. Kabiru Faruk. (*scrolls his phone for the text message*) I received this message from him few minutes ago on my way coming here (*Reads*) "Class chairman inform the class that the 30% Continuous Assessment test comes up immediately after the lecture at the E-centre."

CLASS: (*reacts in spontaneous unison*) NOOO! NOOO! We are not ready, NOOO! Not today. NOOO!

CLASS CHAIRMAN: (*agreeing with the class*) Indeed, we are not ready, we've not been informed in good time and today is Monday for crying out loud.

MALE STUDENT 1: Why give us the 30% at a go? Doesn't he know that the abbreviation C.A means CONTINUOUS ASSESSMENT which must be done piece-meal!

FEMALE STUDENT 1: This is his second lecture he will attend since the beginning of the semester, what has he taught us enough even for just 10%; and the exams are coming up in a few weeks' time.

CLASS CHAIRMAN: This is short changing us students, these lecturers must earn their salaries, and Dr Kabiru Faruk has not earned his. We must stand our ground and stop this bogus test until we are taught enough to be examined for. Therefore, in my capacity as the chairman, I declare that there will be no hurried test in this course and certainly not today.

CLASS: (*excitedly*) Chamo! Our great Chamo!! Stop him! Stop him!! (*and gradually the shouts turn to a synchronized chant*) Chamo! Chamo!! Chamo!!! Chamo!!!!

FEMALE STUDENT II: (*Bangs the table*) My mates are you mad, or what are you, have you no sense, manners or maturity but to babble like drunkards this early morning? Now listen to me chairman of lazy students, I am ready for the test midday or midnight, anytime anywhere! As students we must always be ready for learning and examination! You bunch of *fashionistas* and swaggers.

FEMALE STUDENT I: Hey! Lady Shakespeare, do not hide behind Malvolio to insult us, we are not clowns here but clever students. As for fashion and swagger, you must not ignore the fact that some of us are celebrities who made name for the University as a Centre of Excellence in learning and modernization, which includes fashion and beauty. It is unfortunate that villagers like you are also called university students.

FEMALE STUDENT II: My lady *fashionista*, there are celebrities and there are celebrities, some are here for fashion while some are here for knowledge. I am an academic celebrity, my attire and make-up are my brain and books. I am ready for the **TEST**, midday or midnight, here or anywhere!

MALE STUDENT II: Sure, you are ready for the **TASTE** midday or midnight, but for the sake of secrecy and decency let it be at midnight, please.

CLASS CHAIRMAN: Yes! And you can be **TASTED** anywhere but not here in the lecture hall. By midnight this hall will be full of students reading for their exams and continuous assessment tests.

FEMALE STUDENT II: That's all you do, reading for examination not for knowledge; a useless bunch of lazy students! You forget what you have memorized for the e- Exam immediately you log out of the exam.

MALE STUDENT I: And so what? What else do you expect from e-learning and e-Examination, is it not superficial knowledge, learning just to pass the examination?

FEMALE STUDENT II: Do you call that nonsense Examination? Questions that come with their answers and all you need to do is just to click on. In e-Exam you use your fingers not your brain, is either you know the answer or you guess it. Bring a first year student of French to the examination hall for final year Medical students, there is a high possibility that he can guess correctly in most of the questions and pass the course with a good grade.

CLASS CHAIRMAN: That is the point! If your brain doesn't have the answers, guess with your fingers; *Allah nuna min gidan gaskiya-* Click! (*repeat three times*) Chances are you will click in all correctly.

MALE TUDENT II: Chamo, please do not let this *agent provocateur* distract us from our rightful course, Dr Faruk has taught us nothing and has nothing to examine us for. We are here certainly to learn but not to be rushed. If it were so, we wouldn't stay for four years to get a degree, it can be done in four months if all lecturers were to rush us the way he is doing.

MALE STUDENT I: All we are saying, no teaching no test. *Simpliciter.*

CLASS CHAIRMAN: And I dare say, no cheating in teaching.

Enter Zakinatu Joji, a sybaritic female student popular among her course mates for her gregariousness and derring-do. She enters the hall almost running but on noticing that there is no lecturer in the class, she calms down with a poise. The class did not respond as they would do ordinarily, but she is not disappointed. She walks to the rostrum and switches on the electronic board. She pulls out the electronic board marker and writes on the board: ENG 406- PRACTICAL PHONETICS. She then turns to face the class once more, pretending to be the lecturer but then notices the pensive mood of her classmates.

ZAKINATU JOJI: Hi! Folks, why the doldrums this morning? I know you don't enjoy phonetics but not to worry, Zaky Baby is teaching you **Pornetics** today and I promise is gonna be damn well **porn.** (*Stressing the words 'pornetics' and 'porn' to mimic the course lecturer's phonological deformity with plosives and fricatives*).

CLASS CHAIRMAN: Come on! Zaky. The only thing you can do to get us out of this doldrums is to stop DR. Faruk from conducting his so-called 30% C.A Test today.

MALE STUDENT I: That's it. Zaky Baby, please remain there until he comes in, then you can use your seductive ways with men to confuse him and make him forget both the lecture and the nonsense C.A. Test.

MALE STUDENT II: Sure! And we will be your backup artistes while you rap him with your seductive phonetics. (*Mimics her speaking romantically with affected accent*). 'Ex-kiss me Sir...about the taste Sir, I mean the C.A Test Sir...

ZAKINATU JOJI: Hold it folks, what bullshit test are you talking about? I'm not ready for it. This is Monday morning and Zaky baby is still in a hangover from the week-end bashes (*she does some backsliding dance steps to cheer up the class*)

FEMALE STUDENT I: As for me, is not just the hangover that is weighing me down, I need to be at the saloon immediately after this lecture to make my hair. I have a birthday bash tonight at the Pyramid and I need to look kinky. Please, Zaky this man must not spoil my day with his silly E-Test.

CLASS: Zaky baby stop him! Zaky love, seduce him! NO test today, NO test tomorrow, NO test at all!

ZAKINATU JOJI: Relax babes, guys chill. Trust me with the power of seduction, and DR. Faruk is not a Saint for that matter. After all, I was together with him at the Spinsters Club last night. He may be having his own dose of hangover as well, he may not even be here for the lecture.

FEMALE STUDENT II: The devil take your souls! There comes the lecturer you lazy students.

Zakinatu quickly takes a seat in the front row and the whole class goes dead silent. DR. Kabiru Faruk enters the lecture hall rather vivaciously, his mood is obviously pleasant which assuages the students apprehension and suits Zakinatu's seduction strategy.

ZAKINATU JOJI: (*sitting in the front she takes advantage of proximity and mood of the lecturer to entice him with seductive smiles and suggestive comments*) You look

pornographically sweet this morning Sir, we will sure enjoy **pornetics** with you today.

DR. KABIRU FARUK: Zakinatu, zhere is nothing **pfhotographic** about me this morning, and I wonder how zhat can make you enjoy phonetics today.

ZAKINATU JOJI: I speak for the class Sir, and for the spinsters at the Club.

DR. KABIRU FARUK: O! Yes, zhe Spinsters Club...Sorry, I mean... yes, did you say pfhotographs or...

ZAKINATU JOJI: (*smiling suggestively*) yes the pornographs, no, the pfhotographs, sorry... the Test...

DR. KABIRU FARUK: Yes, zhe Test after zhe class, I remember...

ZAKINATU JOJI: No Sir, the TASTE yesterday, at the club... Yes Sir, the Test today... No Sir...another day Sir...

DR. KABIRU FARUK: Another day did you say?

CLASS: Yes Sir, another day, the E-Test... We are not ready.

FEMALE STUDENT II: I'm ready Sir, I'm ready today, even here and now.

DR. KABIRU FARUK: Ready for what, zhe E-Test or...?

MALE STUDENT II: Yes Sir, she's ready for pornetics class

CLASS: Yes Sir! Pornetics class, No C.A Test sir, teach us pornetics and **pornology** sir!

DR. KABIRU FARUK: Hold it! Hold it! I have heard you let's get started. (*He goes to the board and finds a topic already written there.)* Good! We have already started Pornetics. What do you understand by zhe term Phonetics? (*Pronounces it like pornetics*)

ZAKINATU JOJI: (*shoots up her hand and was already on her feet even before DR. Faruk recognizes her*)

DR. KABIRU FARUK: Yes Zakinatu, let's hear you.

ZAKINATU JOJI: Escuse me Sir, (*Pronounces the word deliberately to sound like Es-squeeze*) do you mean "Phonetics" as written on the board or "Pornetics" as you pronounced it Sir?

DR. KABIRU FARUK: Before I answer you my zdear, (*Zaky blushes*) you must get zhe correct pronunciation of zhe word "Excuse"----Es-cuse, two syllables not "Es-sque-eze", three syllables. Now back to Pornetics...

ZAKINATU JOJI: Thank you Sir. Pornetics sir is the science and practice of pornology otherwise called pornocracy.

DR. KABIRU FARUK: Preposterous! absolute balderdash (*and then smiles knowingly*). My zdear girl (*Zaky again responds to the use of "My" on her knowingly by waving her hand at the class with a smile*) you are mixing words in a dangerous way. Pornetics and Pornocracy are two diametrically opposed terms, Infact, zhe word **Pornocracy** is an irresponsible word meaning a government by "pfrostitutes" or dominated by "pfrostitutes". (*Stressing on the word **prostitutes**).*

ZAKINATU JOJI: That's our government Sir, a government by political prostitutes.

DR. KABIRU FARUK: NO, my dear you are digressing, get back to zhe topic-"pornetics"

CHAIRMAN: Sir, let me assist her with the definition.

DR. KABIRU FARUK: Yes, Class Chairman.

CHAIRMAN: Phonetics is the science of sounds and how they function in language.

DR. KABIRU FARUK: Good! bvery good. Class do you understand? And my zdear girl, is zhat understood?

ZAKINATU JOJI: Yes, my dear sir, it's very clear now sir.

DR. KABIRU FARUK: O.K, class who can give me an exampfle of a sound in English.

ZAKINATU JOJI: I'm still on my feet sir, how do you want it, practical or written?

DR. KABIRU FARUK: Pfractical, of course.

ZAKINATU JOJI: (*without waiting for the lecturer to end his statement, she jumps over the table to the front and stands facing the lecturer. She then makes a sound "ptch!" pouting her mouth at the lecturer as if she would spit the sound straight into his mouth*).

DR. KABIRU FARUK: (*Smiling with surprise*) what's zhat, pfouting at me as if we are in a romance class.

ZAKINATU JOJI: You asked me to give it to you sir, practical, like a kiss.

DR. KABIRU FARUK: Alright! I heard you. Now can you tell me, or anyone of you in zhe class, what type of sound is zhat in pornetics?

ZAKINATU JOJI: I am still standing by sir, I can tell you. It is called bi-labial sound, sir.

DR. KABIRU FARUK: Good, Zakinatu. Can you now expflain to the class how bi-labial sound is realized in spfeech?

ZAKINATU JOJI: Bi-labial sound is realized in speech when two lips come together in a swift or fixed contact as is done in kissing, sir.

DR. KABIRU FARUK: Kissing! How do you mean?

ZAKINATU JOJI: (*Taking the lecture by surprise, she swiftly lands a snap kiss on his lips with the sound* **ptch** *made deliberately loud*) This is how to kiss sir (*she uses her right thumb to clean the patch of red lipstick on his lisps. The class burst into guffaws and giggles, obviously enjoying Zakinatu's strategies of seduction*)

DR. KABIRU FARUK: (*Feigning embarrassment*) Young lady, do you understand what you have just done?

ZAKINATU JOJI: Yes, I do sir. That was a bi-labial voiced sound. If we are to repeat the contact and keep it much longer, that one is called bi-labial voiceless sound. (*She jumps at him once again with another hot kiss, this time holding his head by the cheeks to ensure their mouths remained steadily glued together much longer*)

As DR. Faruk struggles to free himself from her romantic grips, even though effortlessly, the class too is agog with excitement even as they vocalize the voiceless action by licking their lips loudly to make the kissing sound. DR. Faruk eventually extricates himself from Zakinatu's grips and hurries out of the class leaving the students enjoying themselves at his expense as they sing and dance.

BLACK OUT

MOVEMENT TWO

CLASS CHAIRMAN: Zaky you are a witch! Did you see the large patch of red you left on his mouth? Poor man, I wonder what sort of sensation he is creating out there on his way to the office.

MALE STUDENT II: It would be worse for him if he rushes back to the house from here with that kind of mouth.

ZAKINATU JOJI: Rush to which house, he's going nowhere. He must be there waiting for me in his office, he is expecting a follow up. I'm not done with him yet! (*She brings out a lipstick and a small mirror from her handbag. She stands before the class and applies the lipstick lavishly on her mouth. She admires herself briefly in the mirror and does the sign of kissing by pouting her mouth at the class*) I'm going after him, enjoy yourselves here while I do mine there.

CLASS CHAIRMAN: Very well, Zaky Baby, rush after him and make him forget about the C.A. test forever.

ZAKINATU JOJI: Chamo, by the time I'm done with him he would not only forget the test forever but he would have also given me the softcopy of the E-exam questions.

CLASS: Zaky! Zaky! Zaky! (*She cat walks out of the class*)

CLASS CHAIRMAN: Colleagues, Course mates, comrades, lend me your ears once more. What has just transpired between Zaky and DR. Faruk is called professional hazard. ASUU has always insisted that lecturers teaching hazardous courses should be paid handsome hazard allowance for the risk involved in the job. You can now see the emotional risk involved in teaching practical Phonetics.

MALE STUDENT I: Mr. Chairman, if that is professional hazard which must attract handsome allowance, I'm coming back to the University after my graduation just to teach practical phonetics, and enjoy all the hazards without asking for any allowance.

FEMALE STUDENT I: The hazard allowance should in all fairness be given to the female students in the course and not the lecturer. Zaky took a great risk by kissing DR. Faruk in the name of practical phonetics. DR. Faruk could have bitten off her lips and nose in his covetousness.

MALE STUDENT II: What happened between Zaky and DR. Faruk is called Sexual Harassment not professional hazard.

FEMALE STUDENT II: Who was harassing who then in this case? Certainly, it was Zaky with her derring-do and libidinous conduct that was harassing the innocent lecturer.

FEMALE STUDENT I: It may as well be a fringe benefit for the lecturer. I'm sure DR. Faruk enjoyed listening to Zaky's kissing sounds on his lips more than he would like to hear the dull plosive sounds drop on his ears.

MALE STUDENT I: Sexual Harassment, Professional Hazard, Fringe Benefit, Seduction or whatever you may call it, these risks are not only in language classes but also common in literature, especially in Poetry, Creative Writing and Theatre Workshop where everything is practical.

CLASS CHAIRMAN: And practically speaking, the phonetics class is over and I can see DR. Kimaram Tiwe coming for Poetry.

Chairman quickly leaves the rostrum to take his seat among his colleagues. Dead silence falls on the class as they remain orderly waiting for DR. Kimaram to enter. He enters the class to find the students in an excited mood, which gives him the flip to plunge straight into the lecture.

DR. KIMARAM TIWE: Last week we discussed the nature of Romantic Poetry. We concluded that the poetry is imbued with emotional naturalism, that romantic poetry appeals to feeling and demonstrates the healthy effect of instinctual life. We have listed poets such as D.H. Lawrence, William Blake, William Wordsmith, Samuel T. Coleridge, P.B Shelly and John Keats among renown older English romantics. I have assigned you to study them and the other newer poets. Today I will be listening to you perform the poems you have studied and explain the effects they had on you.

BUKAR KAKA: *(raising his hand before any other person)*

DR. KIMARAM TIWE: Yes, Bukar...I understand that your mates call you B.K. romance, why if I may ask?

BUKAR KAKA: Yes, Sir. It's due to my romantic sensibility Sir. I read the poem "Piano" by D.H Lawrence, sir.

DR. KIMARAM TIWE: Go on, let's hear you.

BUKAR KAKA: (*reads*)

> Softly, in the dusk,
>
> A woman is singing for me
>
> Taking me back
>
> Down the vistas of years..."

DR. KIMARAM TIWE: (*Cuts him off*) Good, hold it there. Next... ok you at the back.

LADI LAMBA: I read the poem "Go, Lovely Rose" by Edmund Waller, it is a romantic counsel to young ladies like me.

DR. KIMARAM TIWE: Good to know, give us the poem in part.

LADI LAMBA: (*reads with seductive gestures and smiles*)

> "Go, lovely Rose_
>
> Tell her that wastes her time and me,
>
> When I resemble her to thee,
>
> How sweet and fair she seems to be..."

(*DR. Tiwe joins her to the next stanza by heart*)

DR. TIWE/LADI: "Tell her that's young

> And shuns to have her graces spied,

> That hadst though sprang

> In deserts where no man abide

> Thou must have uncommented died...

> *(She collapses in Dr. Tiwe's arms, he fondles her briefly)*

DR. KIMARAM TIWE: Well done! Well done! What lesson does the poem teach you?

LADI LAMBA: It teaches me to do things at the right time, to make hay while the sun shines, to seize the day and display my beauty *(she displays her beauty and shape seductively).*

DR. KIMARAM TIWE: Excellent! Hold it! Keep it for now. Next person!. Yes, Rose.

ROSE LOSHIN: The title of my poem is "Song of Solomon" and is addressed to me.

DR. KIMARAM TIWE: Who wrote the poem?

ROSE LOSHIN: King Solomon himself!

DR. KIMARAM TIWE: King Solomon wrote you a poem, was it posthumously or you lived in his time?

ROSE LOSHIN: The poem is addressed to the flower "rose" among other precious things of nature. I here personify the flower as a creation of nature.

DR. KIMARAM TIWE: Let's hear you Lady Rose.

ROSE LOSHIN: (*Reads poem with theatricality, demonstrating every attribute with exaggerated gesture.*)

"I am the rose of Sharon,

And the lily of the valleys.

As the lily among the thorns,

So is my love among the girls.

As the apple tree among the trees of the forest,

So is my beloved among the boys

I sat down under his shadows with great delight,

And his fruit was sweet to my taste.

He brought me to the banqueting house

And his banner over me was love" ...

Cut! Hold it there.

DR. KIMARAM TIWE: (*At the point he cuts her off she was already in front of him, seemingly unconsciously as she was dancing all through as she performs the poem. DR. Tiwe who also knows the poem by heart, and is flowing with her as she glides with the lines, now completes the stanza for her.*)

"Stay me with flogans, comfort me with apples: For I am sick of love".

(*Rose collapses in his arms, class goes into a wild and excited roar, some cuddling each other to compliment the main actors*).

SANUSI MUHAMMED: (*stands up and walks to the front without any invitation*). Excuse me sir, I've a more exciting poem but I'd need a female partner to read to.

DR. KIMARAM TIWE: What is the title and by who?

SANUSI MUHAMMED: The poem is titled "Her Breasts" written by Nizar Kabbani.

DR. KIMARAM TIWE: Oh! The sensuous and romantic Arab poet who gave voice to the emotionally suppressed Arab women of his time. Let's hear him.

MARY SHAMKONG: (*stands up and walks to the front*) I here stand proxy for the owner of the breasts. (*she cuddles her voluptuous breasts for emphasis*)

CLASS: (*claps for Mary Shamkong*)

SANUSI MUHAMMED: (*Reads*) Unlock the treasury! (*Mary does the sign of opening her breast*)

Lay bare your burning breasts (*She reveals the cleavage*)

Don't smother your imprisoned fire (*She cuddles the lobes*)

Your breasts are the two most beautiful paintings

Two balls of silk spun by the generous morning

So come close to me my little cat, (*She comes close*)

Let yourself free

Come close. (*She gets much close* He stretches his hands to pull her much closer).

(he stretches his hands to pull her closer)

Think of the fate of your breasts

With the turning of the seasons.

Don't panic. (*Tries to fiddle with her breasts then to the audience*)

Foolish is she who hides her breasts

And let her youth pass without being kissed.

(*He now grabs her, enfolds her completely in his arms*)

DR. KIMARAM TIWE: Good, you can let go of her now and answer me. Who does the poem remind you among the English romantic poets?

SUNUSI MUHAMMED: It reminds me of the poem, "To His Coy Mistress" by Andrew Marvel

DR. KIMARAM TIWE: Good!

MARY SHAMKONG: The poem gives similar counsel to that of Edmund Waller's "Go ye, Lovely Rose"

DR. KIMARAM TIWE: Correct, my dear! You're very right.

(*Another female student shots up her hand to present another poem*) Yes, you there, the Lady in Pink. What's your name?

PINK LADY: My name is long sir we need to be very close for you to get it, I think "Pink Lady" is a romantic English version of my name sir, I accept it.

DR. KIMARAM TIWE: So henceforth you are Pink Lady.

PINK LADY: In the spirit of romantic poetry and lack of close contact, yes sir.

DR. KIMARAM TIWE: Yes, Pink Lady, what is the title of your poem?

PINK LADY: (*She stands up, adjusts her dress around the chest to reveal more of her cleavage. She steals quick glances at the class, fixing squint look at the lecturer and then replies)* "I love you"

DR. KIMARAM TIWE: What! Are you sure?

PINK LADY: Very sure, Sir.

DR. KIMARAM TIWE: I mean the title not the statement.

PINK LADY: Yes, either way Sir.

DR. KIMARAM TIWE: Who wrote the poem?

PINK LADY: The name is too long sir, you need to see it to get it sir.

DR. KIMARAM TIWE: Right let's have the poem then.

PINK LADY: Not here sir, I will give you after class.

DR. KIMARAM TIWE: Well Lady 'I love you'...

PINK LADY: (*Cuts in quickly, deliberately)* Thank you Sir, I love you too Sir.

DR. KIMARAM TIWE: I mean the title of your poem not a compliment, my dear.

PINK LADY: Yes my dear, sorry, yes sir. Either way is the same thing, Sir.

DR. KIMARAM TIWE: Pink Lady, you are obviously a good material for romantic poetry yourself.

PINK LADY: I'm all flowers and fragrances with romantic sensibilities, I stand proxy for the poem sir. You may want to observe me for that sir.

DR. KIMARAM TIWE: Well class, I think our Pink Lady would make a good human laboratory for the observation and appreciation of nature, and as an object of creative writing. We should end this class on a romantic note by inviting our Pink Lady to come forward and give us a 3DG poise and posture for our romantic delight and inspiration for poetic imagination.

(*Pink Lady walks seductively to the front of the class and gives several romantic poises and postures for the admiration of the class and the seduction of the Lecturer. The class cheers her up and spontaneously breaks loose in lewd dance steps that envelop her. Music plays as they dance.*

BLACK OUT

MOVEMENT THREE

Action resumes in DR. Faruk's office. Zakinatu enters not long after DR. Faruk arrives from the class.

DR. KABIRU FARUK: Zakinatu! You were on my heels; I've just entered zhe oppice.

ZAKINATU JOJI: (*seductively*) Sir, you left the class unceremoniously, the students have asked me to follow you immediately to express their concern.

DR. KABIRU FARUK: Today's lecture was excepftional, I hope you all enjoyed it.

ZAKINATU JOJI: The lecture was the best so far. I hope we get this type of practical teaching in the examination too.

DR. KABIRU FARUK: Zhe examination is done electronically, not pfractically. We can only have it in a Continuous Assessment Test and lecture period...

ZAKINATU JOJI: (*Cuts in*) and in the office too, Sir.

DR. KABIRU FARUK: Yes in zhe oppice too as Continuous Assessment Test, one-on-one.

ZAKINATU JOJI: Oh! That reminds me, you forgot about the C.A Test at the E-centre.

DR. KABIRU FARUK: Yes... Yes... zhe C.A test apfter zhe class, I compfletely forgot about it. How exciting zhe class was!

ZAKINATU JOJI: You said C.A test is possible in the office, one on one. We can as well have the **TASTE** here instead of going to the E-centre. You can start with me right away, I'm ready sir.

DR. KABIRU FARUK: Well, you know pornology is like opfhthalmology, zhey need close contact- mouth to mouth, eye ball to eye ball.

ZAKINATU JOJI: (*Moves closer to DR. Faruk*) I think we are close enough sir, one on one. Shall we then, I'm ready.

DR. KABIRU FARUK: Which word do you want to be tested on?

ZAKINATU JOJI: I want to be **TASTED** for the "F" word, Sir.

DR. KABIRU FARUK: Zhe "F" word! What do you mean?

ZAKINATU JOJI: Yes sir. I mean the Fricatives.

DR. KABIRU FARUK: Oh! Zhe pfricatives, I understand you. I hope you have a sweet tongue, pfricatives are by nature pfrictions which zhe tongue must lubricate as in zhe F sound (*he kisses her to demonstrate how the sound is made*). Zhis is called labio-dental pfricative sound as in zhe word "pfork"

ZAKINATU JOJI: (*pretending to hear the word as fuck*) "Fuck", sir?

DR. KABIRU FARUK: Yes, as in pfork and knife.

ZAKINATU JOJI: Oh! Now I understand the pronunciation, sir.

DR. KABIRU FARUK: Good. Another exampfle is the sound 'S'. a pfricative sound called inter-dental pfricative.

ZAKINATU JOJI: 'S' as in the word...

DR. KABIRU FARUK: (*Cuts her off*)... As in zhe word sex...

ZAKINATU JOJI: (*also cuts him off knowingly*)... I know sir, as in the word sexy!.

DR. KABIRU FARUK: No! I mean as in zhe word sexagenarian, like me.

ZAKINATU JOJI: Yes sir, sexy for a female like me, and sexagenarian for a male like you.

DR. KABIRU FARUK: How clever! No my dear. Sexagenarian means a person who is sixty years old, like me. It is from zhe word "six" not "sex"- sixty not sexy.

ZAKINATU JOJI: But the letter S in both "sexagenarian" and "sexy" is followed by "E" not "I", sir. Therefore, phonologically and logically the root of the word should be "sex" not "six"!

DR. KABIRU FARUK: Zhat is zhe absurdity of zhe English language; zheir grammatical rules are not amenable to logic.

ZAKINATU JOJI: Let's get back to fricatives sir, mouth to mouth, what role does the tongue play in fricative sounds sir, apart from lubrication?

DR. KABIRU FARUK: (*Knowingly*) zhe tongue is used to taste zhe sound.

ZAKINATU JOJI: TASTE, how sir?, I mean practically speaking?

DR. KABIRU FARUK: Don't know how? Come closer (*Zakinatu gets much closer*) bring out your tongue (*She brings out the whole of her tongue. DR. Faruk does the same, their tongues tasting each other's. Then both grab each other's cheeks as they get themselves drowned in a bout of kisses*).

BLACK OUT

MOVEMENT FOUR

DR. Faruk now goes back home from the office with conspicuously red lips like bleeding. His wife is quick to notice.

MRS LAMI KABIRU: My dear, did you have a boxing bout at the office today?

DR. KABIRU FARUK: Why, how do you mean?

MRS LAMI KABIRU: Your mouth is all red with blood, the lips look like bleeding.

DR. KABIRU FARUK: Blood! *(Alarmed, he touches the lips and notices traces of red lipstick)* Oh!, lipfstick.

MRS LAMI KABIRU: *(Flabbergasted)* lipstick! How come?

DR. KABIRU FARUK: Don't you know I teach **Pornetics** and **pornology** to a class dominated by pfemale students? Today's lecture was on bi-labial sounds.

MRS LAMI KABIRU: I should be the one to remind you that I majored in English with First Class, my final year project was on phonetics. I have never come across in both teaching and research where lipsticks are used to teach bi-labial sounds.

DR. KABIRU FARUK: Zhat was zhen, my zdear wife, when teaching was analogue. Today we do E-Teaching and Examination. Pfart of E-teaching is to use natural audio-bvisual aids, pfor pornetics we use our lipfs to demonstrate how sounds are made. Zhe lipfstick on my lipfs must be pfrom one of zhe pfemale students I used to illustrate zhe nature of bi-labial sounds. How careless I was, I should have washed my mouth apfter zhe class, I'm sorry zdarling.

MRS LAMI KABIRU: So, you bring your lips together with a female student's own to teach the class how bi-labial sound is realized?

DR. KABIRU FARUK: Most certainly, yes. Zis is called E-teaching; it just haffened zhat zhe pfarticular student had too much lipfstick on her lipfs. Unlike students of your days who have more time pfor studies zhan pfor pfashion, students zhese days are more of pfashionistas zhan students.

MRS LAMI KABIRU: And the teachers too, they are more of lechers than lecturers, right?

ZAKINATU JOJI: (*Comes rushing into the house*) Good morning madam. I'm sorry to rush in like that. Excuse me sir, I'm sorry to follow you home but I left a lot of lipstick on your lips, I need to retrieve some to reinforce my own. (*She grabs Dr. Forbun, rubbing her mouth all over his own to get her lips more colour*)

DR. KABIRU FARUK: (*unabashed*) My zdear wife, what she has just done is called bi-labial voiceless sound, if you remember your pornetics. Now let's show you how bi-labial voiced sound is made (*Dr. Forbun also grabs Zakinatu kissing her noisily*)

MRS LAMI KABIRU: (*To the audience*) Now I understand how the coinage **Pornology** comes into Phonetics, and the havoc E-teaching and E-examination are doing to modern Education. Bi-labial sound in E-learning means bringing together the lips of a female student and a male lecturer to produce voiceless orgasms.

DR. KABIRU FARUK: Exactly! my zdear wife. You certainly made a First Class in English. How I wish you were employed to teach pornetics instead of your current job as frotocol opficer to the Vice-Chancellor.

MRS LAMI KABIRU: That is not the point we are discussing, tell me more about the E-exam. What will be the options of answer to this question on lipstick phonetics?

ZAKINATU JOJI: Aunty, that is very simple, the options are in the taste of the lipstick- (a) vanilla (b) strawberry (c) pineapple... it all depends on the taste the lipstick leaves on the tongue of the lecturer. As for this particular exercise the answer is obviously (b) strawberry, that is the taste of my lipstick.

MRS LAMI KABIRU: Did you say the taste is like strawberry, have you ever tasted that of caneberry as well?

ZAKINATU JOJI: No Aunty, how nice does it taste?

MRS LAMI KABIRU: Don't know how nice?, wait a minute. (*She dashes into the house and comes out with a big strong cane and rained lashes on Zakinatu, serrating her* *all over the body. Zakinatu runs out screaming and cursing Dr. Faruk for watching without help.*

BLACK OUT

MOVEMENT FIVE

At the Students' Centre. A group of students are seen in the Common Room relaxing with bottles of soft drinks and snacks. Among them are students from the Department English sharing their experience of the morning's lecture with other students from other faculties. Agnes James, a female student from the Faculty of Science now speaks.

AGNES JAMES: Why do you focus so much on the English department, these techniques are also common in Science classes, especially in Human Anatomy.

YUSUF YAKONG: Yes, I remember a story from the campus magazine, that was...eh...GQ Magazine. It carried a story of a practical class in human Anatomy where a female student was used as a specimen for lack of cadaver.

CHUKWUDE IGWE: That was last year when the University was hard hit by the Single Treasury Account Syndrome. The college needed a cadaver for emergency practical and there was no money immediately to buy a dead body. Therefore some students volunteered themselves for the practical.

AGNES JAMES: Hold it!, you only read about it in the flimsy campus magazine. I was a participant observer, it happened in my class. The use of "life cadavers" as we called the volunteers was not as a necessity but a novelty. The lecturer wanted to experiment with human beings as a form of E-teaching; but it was more fun than learning.

YUSUF YAKONG: Tell us more since you were part of it, did you play the cadaver or just the observer?

AGNES JAMES: The fun was on the life cadaver and the lecturer, Dr. Ayodele John; the rest of us were just crazy with excitement. Those of you in the Department of English should bring out a good comedy drama from the story.

MARY SHAMKONG: Give us the details, I will play the cadaver.

SANUSI MOHAMMED: And I will play the course lecturer, it's another fringe benefit for me to play with Mary's supple body again.

AGNES JAMES: And the rest of us will play the students, I will especially be elated to re-live the experience.

MARY SHAMKONG: Come on folks, let's listen to the details and hold an emergency rehearsal to act out the incidence.

Agnes explains the incidence mimetically, while they set up the table for the practical. Mary Shamkong is taken and laid on the table. The rest surround her as students listening to Sanusi Muhammed now acting as Dr. Ayodele, the lecturer.

DR. AYODELE JOHN: The human body has three very important external parts (*He adjusts Mary's position on the table by removing her hands on the chest and* *placing them by her sides)*. The first part is the face which has on it two very important features namely, the eyes and the lips.

CHUKWUDE IGWE: What of the ears and the nose sir, are they not important?

DR. AYODELE JOHN: Those are for hearing and smelling, they cannot be more important than the eyes and lips especially that our specimen here is a female. The first sensational contact is with the eyes and the best taste of the pudding is on the lips. Once these upper outer organs are secured, what is hidden below is just there waiting for you.

CADAVER: Sir, my lips are thirsty for the taste.

DR. AYODELE JOHN: Shut up! Cadavers don't talk. Let me finish the labelling. The other important parts are the chest and what is below the waist.

YUSUF YAKONG: The chest is all bones sir, and atimes hairy.

DR. AYODELE JOHN: That is for a male student, nobody needs you for practicals. (*points at Mary's erect breasts)* what did you see here?

YUSUF YAKONG: Two firm, erect, conical shape chunks of flesh on the chest (*Demonstrates the shape excitedly with his hands and fingers.)*

DR. AYODELE JOHN: These succulent moulds of meat are called breasts, the source of pleasure and objects of fancy. We need to understand the vulnerability of the breasts to diseases, especially cancer. The human body is a complex system of tissues, nerves and glands. The breast is full of tissues hence its vulnerability to cancer.

YUSUF YAKONG: How does cancer manifest itself, Sir?

DR. AYODELE JOHN: Cancer, otherwise called neoplasia, is a disease in which the cells of a tissue undergo uncontrolled and rapid proliferation. There are different types of cancer but the most common among women are breast cancer and cervical cancer. Today we will be looking at breast cancer.

CHUKWUDE IGWE: Are men not liable to cancer, Sir?

DR. AYODELE JOHN: They are of course, especially prostate cancer. But for the purpose of practical anatomy, the female organs are more exciting to teach.

AGNES JAMES: Why so, Sir?

DR. AYODELE JOHN: Don't know why? First of all, to prevent breast cancer for instance scientist encourages the sucking of the breast. Secondly, to detect cancer you need to fiddle with the breast, touch it, squeeze it, massage it, oh! What a pleasure to teach it. As a lifeless cadaver, just a touch of the nipples will bring ripples of life to the dead body. (*He touches Mary's nipple, she shakes with sensation, he touches the other she reacts the same way*)

The students then take turns in touching her nipples. When the hand is that of a male, she responds with sensuous spasm, if it is that of a female she remains lifeless. This continues in turns repeatedly as they have fun doing so. Sanusi now attempts sucking her breast which made her get up abruptly. They are all laughing boisterously, taking toasts with their soft drink bottles, celebrating Mary's rising from the dead. Enter another female student.

HAUWA IBRAHIM: Hi! guys what are we celebrating without advertising; this vivacious group of soon-to-graduate gurus?

MARY SHAMKONG: We are celebrating my return to life after being a cadaver in the Human Anatomy laboratory for today's lecture.

HAUWA IBRAHIM: Oh! You were used as specimen for practical anatomy? How innovative the lecturer was.

MARY SHAMKONG: Not the whole of me, the lecturer was interested in my breasts only.

AGNES JAMES: Actually he started with the eyes, stressing on the way the eyes dilate with pleasure each time they sight a beautiful girl.

HAUWA IBRAHIM: The eyes again? I just had my own share of the trials of the eyes at the ophthalmology department.

AGNES JAMES: Another practical examination?

HAUWA IBRAHIM: No, another e-test of my ability to read pornographic words.

MARY SHAMKONG: The ophthalmologist must have titillated you in order to dilate the eyes to read the words *pornotically* as is done in *pornetics* class.

HAUWA IBRAHIM: It was more than titillation; it was a romantic display of the theatre of the absurd.

YUSUF YAKONG: Another drama, it seems we have more theatre in the Sciences than in the Arts.

HAUWA IBRAHIM: These Doctors are terrible, they have turned their offices into operating theatre where they do all manners of operation. I went there to complain about my right eyes which twitches and itches constantly these days. And guess what happened, Dr. Effiong Okot nearly raped me in the name of e-Examination of my eyes. We need to act it for you to visualize my trials.

SANUSI MUHAMMED: I have just acted a doctor for the anatomy class, let me act the doctor for the ophthalmology theatre. Give me the details and I will take over the action.

Lamila mimes the story to him while the rest listen along. He suddenly assumes the role of Actor/Director explaining to Lamila what to do in the pantomime.

SANUSI MUHAMMED: Silence please, I need your attention. We are now transiting from Anatomy to Ophthalmology in our study of the art of Seduction in e-Teaching and e-Examinattion in our e-compliant University. I therefore play the role of Dr. Effiong Okot of the Ophthalmology Department, Lamila is my specimen for the practical.

DR. EFFONG OKOT: (*Sanusi now acting as Dr. Effiong the Ophthalmologist*) Look here, young lady (*He writes the word "YOU" on the white board*) close your right eye and read what is on the board

HAUWA IBRAHIM: (*Reads*) "YOU"

DR. EFFONG OKOT: (*Writes the word "AND"*) close your left eye and read the next word.

HAUWA IBRAHIM: (*Reads*) "AND"

DR. EFFONG OKOT: (*Writes"I" and asks her to close her right eye again and read*)

HAUWA IBRAHIM: (*Reads*) "I"

DR. EFFONG OKOT: Good, now close your two eyes and read the next writing. (*He writes*) "YOU-AND-I-ARE-IN-LOVE"

HAUWA IBRAHIM: (*She strains her face with closed eyes to read. She bends forward trying hard to read the sentence*) No, I can't see with my eyes closed.

DR. EFFONG OKOT: What! You cannot see the most important words on the board? Then you are finished, you are suffering from blespharospasm, a precursor of irreversible blindness, it's just a matter of time before you go completely blind. I give you one more chance to save yourself from going completely blind. One last chance- READ!

HAUWA IBRAHIM: (*Frightened by the prospect of blindness, she opens one eye partially and reluctantly reads*) WE-ARE-IN-LL...--...LOVE.

DR. EFFONG OKOT: Good! Beautiful! Now come over here for a proper e-examination of your eyes. (*She sits very close to him on a flexible chair that reclines backward*)

Dr. Effiong stands over her with legs astride. He bends down on her to adjust the back of her seat downwards. With a pencil torch light in his hand he beams it on her eyes. He keeps adjusting her chair downwards while he also keeps bending further down on her, until she is virtually lying down face up on the chair while he is also virtually slouching on her. As he pries into her eyes with the sharp, thin light, he brings his face so close to her that their noses and lips are almost rubbing each other.

HAUWA IBRAHIM: (*Stands up abruptly, almost knocking his face with her forehead*). Excuse me Doctor, I didn't know that the procedure involves nose rubbing, lip tasting and slouching on the patient. I need to go and prepare better for you, the perfume I'm wearing is not seductive enough and I will need a tastier lipstick. But meanwhile have this before I go (*She lands a heavy slap on Sanusi's face and they burst with laughter at his expense.*)

BLACK OUT

MOVEMENT SIX

At the female hostel. Zakinatu storms into her room wearing the cane marks on her face and shoulders. She looks furious and distraught. Her roommates express shock and disbelief over her appearance.

ROOM-MATE I: Zaky Baby! What's the matter, you look battered?

ROOM-MATE II: Tell us, who the hell on this campus would dare lay his/her ugly fingers on the beautiful face of the Campus First Lady?

ZAKINATU JOJI: Roommates brace up for a show down with that Sheppopotamus Dr. Faruk keeps in his house as a wife.

ROOM-MATE I: What! You mean the Vice-Chancellor's protocol officer did this to you?

ROOM-MATE II: Has the rivalry between the two of you gotten to the level of fighting each other publicly in the office, or where else could the two of you have met?

ZAKINATU JOJI: I went to her house to see her husband, I forgot my handbag in his car and...as you know...there are a lot of exhibits in the bag...

ROOM-MATE I: And so?

ZAKINATU JOJI: She was mad to see me in the house and talking to her husband. Without asking any questions the primitive woman went for a big stick and before I realized what was to happen she had already started beating me rapidly with vengeance.

ROOM-MATE II: Vengeance for what? Have you in any way come between her and her husband, or is she taking it out on you for her lack of luck with her boss?

ZAKINATU JOJI: Dr. Faruk is very intelligent and charismatic, he must have married that thing under a spell. As for her boss, I don't think he ever noticed her as a woman.

ROOM-MATE I: Is it your fault that her husband dotes on you and her boss too has a crush on you? You did not make yourself beautiful, God created you so, and every man knows you are beautiful.

ZAKINATU JOJI: The die is now cast, the Vice-Chancellor must throw her out of that office and have her posted to our hostel as a hall mistress, so that we can torment her emotionally with our sweet sonorous voices talking amorously about our lecturers, including her husband.

ROOM-MATE I: It's a good idea getting her out of that place, being close to the V.C. who sees her every day in the name of official duty gives her an edge over you.

ROOM-MATE II: In a way her being there is to your advantage, she runs errands for you from the V.C. Remember that day he sent her to the Supermarket to buy a plasma T.V. which she delivered personally to you in the Hostel. You think she was happy doing that?

ZAKINATU JOJI: You are right my dear, let her remain there to serve me. (*Her phone rings, it's the V.C. calling her*) Ssssh! *Oga* is calling (*She puts the phone on hands free to impress her room-mates*) Hello! Sweetie-pie

V.C.s VOICE: Hello Zaky Baby, what about dinner tonight?

ZAKINATU JOJI: I'm always prepared for you, a ready menu for your gastronomic desire. Where do I serve you, my master?

V.C.'s VOICCE: At the guest house of course, come through the Western Gate when it is dark. Come with the spare key to enter, there will be no Porters around tonight.

ZAKINATU JOJI: Girls, he must hear about the barbaric action of his so-called Protocol Officer.

ROOM-MATE I: Please Zakinatu, don't forget the invitation to the church endowment fund launch, use your seductive tactics to make him give a huge donation. You know he listens to you more than he would his wife.

ROOM-MATE II: Don't forget to remind him also to be on the alert, the students are seriously warming up for a show down with the university authorities, it could be tomorrow or next but certainly very soon.

ZAKINATU JOJI: I heard you girls, I must dash to the saloon now to garnish myself very well to look like a sumptuous meal for him. Stay awake no matter how late, I will return with goodies and gossip. (*She dashes*

into the bathroom to prime herself up, she picks her hand bag and hurries out.)

BLACK OUT

42

MOVEMENT SEVEN

At the University Freedom Square. Students are gathered chanting slogans, bracing up for a show down with the University authorities, chanting, drumming and dancing frenziedly.

STUDENTS: We no go gree wo, we no go gree V.C. we no go gree,

STUDENT LEADER: We no go gree wo, we no go gree E-Exam we no go gree,

STUDENTS: We no go gree wo, we no go gree V.C. we no go gree,

STUDENT LEADER: We no go gree wo, we no go gree No electricity, we no go gree,

STUDENTS: We no go gree wo, we no go gree V.C. we no go gree,

STUDENT LEADER: We no go gree wo, we no go gree Exploitation of students, we no go gree,

STUDENTS: We no go gree wo, we no go gre V.C. we no go gree...

STUDENT LEADER: We no go gree wo, we no go gree. ASUU cheating in teaching, we no go gree,

STUDENTS: We no go gree wo, we no go gree V.C. we no go gree.

STUDENT LEADER: We no go gree wo, we no go gree Unelected S.U.G. we no go gree,

STUDENTS: We no go gree wo, we no go gree V.C. we no go gree.

STUDENT LEADER: We no go gree wo, we no go gree Leave our girls, we no go gree.

(*Then comes the sonorous voice of the P.R.O*)

P.R.O: Greaaaaaaaaat Nigerian Students!

STUDENTS: (*respond in unison*) Great!

P.R.O: Greaaaaaaaaat Nigerian Students!

STUDENTS: Great!

P.R.O: I want to blast them!

STUDENTS: Blast them!

P.R.O: I want to demolish them!

STUDENTS: Demolish them!

P.R.O: I want to expose them!

STUDENTS: Expose them!

P.R.O: I want to criticize!

STUDENTS: Criticize!

P.R.O: I want to sensitize!

STUDENTS: Sensitize!

P.R.O: I want to conscientize!

STUDENTS: Conscientize!

P.R.O: I want to mobilize!

STUDENTS: Mobilize!

P.R.O: I want to galvanize!

STUDENTS: Galvanize!

P.R.O: *Aluta continua!*

STUDENTS: *Victoria a certa!*

P.R.O: *Aluta continua!*

STUDENTS: *Victoria a certa!*

P.R.O: Any leadership that ignores the yearnings of its youths, especially students, is not only jeopardizing the peace and security of the nation but also putting itself at the risk of running the gauntlet should the students say enough is enough (*Students cheer him up)*

In this University the students are taken for granted by both the administration and the academic staff. The V.C. has become a globetrotter traveling all over the world wasting University resources bringing nothing in return. Lecturers are always traveling visiting all the Universities in the name of part-time teaching neglecting us here where they are employed and paid to teach full time.

We are not allowed to elect our students leaders, instead the administration handpicks for us those they like. Consequently, we have a Student Union Government whose leadership serves the interest of the administration rather than that of the students.

Where is the President of the SUG here in this crowd? He's absent, away in Dubai purchasing furniture for the office of the SUG President. Don't we have excellent furniture makers here in Nigeria? Who gave him the mandate to do so? The students Parliament did not meet to approve the expenses, who then vetted and approved the budget?

Where is the Vice President here in this crowd? Absent! She is away in Ghana attending Miss Africa Beauty Contest, accompanied by the Social Director and some management staff, all at our own expense. Indeed, where is the Treasurer, the custodian of our money? She is on the V.C.'s entourage to Abuja or nestling in the University Guest House. Examinations are fast approaching and we are still battling with erratic power supply, fluctuating and slow internet service, inadequate water supply and lack of good student leaders to speak for us. Our population is approximately fifty thousand, and each student pays one thousand naira every year which is approximately fifty million naira! This money can give us all the comfort we need in the hostel. But where is the money? Enough is enough, we have all this time remained silent while they exploit us, we must now tell the University that to be silent is not to be dumb, it is to refuse to speak; and silence in relation to speech is speech.

(*A thunderous ovation greets him as he steps aside for the next person to speak*)

PARLIAMENT SPEAKER (*On the podium*) As the speaker of the Students Parliament I move the motion of impeachment of the President, the Vice-President and the Treasurer of the SUG for dubious activities and dereliction of responsibilities!

STUDENTS: We concur! We concur!!

PARLIAMENT SPEAKER: To let the University know that our silence is not docility, I move the motion that we march to the house of the Vice-Chancellor with our grievances and tell him that enough is Enough!

STUDENTS: We concur! We concur!!

PARLIAMENT SPEAKER: However, I must caution us about unwholesome conduct. We must guard against the destruction of University property, we must guard against the use of foul language on the Vice – Chancellor, we must carry no dangerous objects, not even olive branches, least they accuse us of carrying AK47 to the V.C.'s house.

STUDENTS: We concur! We concur!!

PARLIAMENT SPEAKER: If we concur we must also conform.

STUDENTS: We concur! We will conform! We concur! We will conform...!

(*Suddenly, the crowd comes up with a protest song as they march towards the V.C.'s house singing:*

STUDENT LEADER: All we are saying, V.C. give us our rights!

STUDENTS: All we are saying, enough is enough!

STUDENT LEADER: All we are saying, ASUU no teaching no exams!

STUDENTS: All we are saying, enough is enough!

STUDENT LEADER: All we are saying, enough is enough!

STUDENTS: All we are saying, enough is enough!

STUDENT LEADER: All we are saying, V.C. give us our rights!

STUDENTS: All we are saying, enough is enough!

STUDENT LEADER: All we are saying ASUU no teaching no exam!

STUDENTS: All we are saying, enough is enough!

STUDENT LEADER: All we are saying, leave S.U.G. alone!

STUDENTS: All we are saying, enough is enough!

As they reach the V.C.'s house they find the gate latched while the security men on duty stand a good distance behind the gate watching and waiting. The students then turn back and head to the V.C.'s Guest House. They have easy entrance as there is only one security man at the gate. However, before they could do any damage to the place a battalion of police men arrive firing rubber bullets in the air and few canisters of teargas. The students disperse but few of them who went right inside the Guest House are arrested, including Zakinatu Joji who is already inside even before the students arrived.

BLACK OUT

MOVEMENT EIGHT

Inside the Senate Chamber, the hall is full of Senators. The V.C. arrives dressed in Academic Gown and traditional turban to mismatch. One of the Senators, Professor Wawa, gives a deafening scream to announce the entrance of the V.C., followed by a ranting of encomiums on him to the chagrin of most of the Senate members.

PROF. WAWA: Let's welcome our ebullient, charismatic, dogmatic, dynamic, intelligent, diligent and youthful Vice-Chancellor. A quintessential leader, erudite academic and architect of the new face of our University; a vice-chancellor per excellence, a friend of students and a choice of every female student, a professor of traditional titles, a professor of partisan politics, a professor extra ordinary and plenipotentiary, a professor of...

VICE CHANCELLOR: (*cuts him courteously*) Thank you Professor Wawa. I appreciate the encomiums that can only come from an erudite orator and a seasoned professor of history like you. Members of the senate I think Professor Wawa deserves a standing ovation for his intellectual acumen in the rendition of valuable history.

SENATORS: (*Stand up reluctantly clapping more in disgust than appreciation*)

VICE CHANCELLOR: Before going into the agenda of the meeting, I want to use my unchallengeable powers as the Vice-Chancellor and Chairman of Senate to unilaterally appoint Professor Wawa as Speaker and Ombudsman of the University and Senate respectively.

SENATORS: Approoooved! Approoved! Approoooved!!! (*Senate members competing for handshake with Prof Wawa*) Congratulations! Congratulation!! Congratulations!!!

VICE CHANCELLOR: Director, Senate and academic matters, please ensure that this appointment is gazetted and circulated before the Golden Jubilee which is in just few days to come.

DIRECTOR SENATE: I have just sent the message to my secretary through e-communication to do just that. I'm sure the circular will be out before the end of the meeting.

VICE CHANCELLOR: Good! Excellent! Now to the substantive business. As you all know this is an emergency senate meeting to review the incident of yesterday, and to assess the preparation made so far for the Golden Jubilee. As for the preparation, the chairman Central Planning Committee of the celebration has already briefed me on that and copies of the report are already in your e-mail. I'm personally satisfied with the level of preparedness and I commend the Chairman for a good job.

DIRECTOR SENATE: It is indeed a thorough job by the Committee. However, there is one important thing the committee has over looked. The V.C. is the Chief Host of the ceremony, but the First Lady also has the responsibility of hosting female dignitaries coming for the occasion. No budget has been made for the office of the First Lady in that direction.

COMMITTEE CHAIRMAN: That's a serious oversight. If the V.C. approves we would review the budget upward by fifty million naira to take care of the office of the First Lady.

VICE CHANCELLOR: It's not entirely my decision. Senate would have to approve the variation in the budget.

SENATORS: Approoooved! Approved!! Approoooved!!!

BURSAR: Mr. Vice-Chancellor sir, considering the fact that the budget for the celebration has been expended, we need to find a suitable sub-head from where we can transfer money to the new budget. May I therefore suggest that we do a virement from the sub-head for Staff Training and Conference Attendance where we have a chunk of money wasting?

SENATORS: Approoooved! Approved! Approoooved!

VICE-CHANCELLOR: In the light of this development I request for senate approval to cancel forthwith all sponsorship of academic conferences till further notice.

SENATORS: Approoooved! Approved! Approoooved!

VICE-CHANCELLOR: Approval endorsed, Bursar please take immediate action. Now to the next item on the agenda, the students protest of yesterday. The Dean Student

Affairs, Professor Lamone Lamang please brief us on the matter.

PROF. LAMONE LAMANG: Mr. Vice-Chancellor sir, Distinguished Senators, Ladies and Gentlemen. Yesterday at about 21:00hrs a handful of disgruntled and misguided students attacked the residence of the Vice-Chancellor, chanting political slogan and carrying posters of one of the politicians in town. Having met the gates of the V.C.'s house locked, they turned their attention to the V.C.'s Guest House where they broke into, looted valuable items and vandalized the place. On hearing the news I quickly mobilized the University Security men to the area and then invited the police to come and be on stand-by. The situation was swiftly brought under control and some arrests were made.

VICE-CHANCELLOR: How many of them were arrested?

PROF. LAMONE LAMANG: Thirteen of them, only one is a female among them and that was the Treasurer of the Student Union Government.

VICE-CHANCELLOR: They are all dismissed from the University... hold on, did you say that the female student is the Treasurer of the S.U.G.?

PROF. LAMONE LAMANG: Yes Sir. That was Zakinatu Joji.

VICE-CHANCELLOR: Release her. Delete her name from the list. She was not among them... she is innocent...a coincidence...

PROF. AMINA GARBA: Mr. Vice-Chancellor Sir, is too early to judge the students. What should be done now is to set up a panel to investigate the matter and the extent of involvement of each person. We may end up with more names from the testimonies of those arrested.

REGISTRAR: Professor Garba is very correct in her observation. Is not enough to punish them and let the matter die down. We need to understand their grievances and the extent of external influence if any. It seems politics is gradually gaining ground here in the University and students have begun to take sides. Politics is like cultism it breeds dangerous division among staff and students.

VICE-CHANCELLOR: I forbid you to compare Politics with Cultism. Are you saying that those of us that aspire for political offices are cultists? That as a University with a whole department for the study of politics, we should not be interested in politics? Registrar, I think you are alone in your opinion.

PROF. AMINA GARBA: He may not be alone in his opinion, sir. Politics as a national discourse concerns us as academics, but partisan politics with its inordinate ambition for power is not worth our while. The Vice-Chancellor may hold a different opinion, but this is the fact.

REGISTRAR: Mr. Vice-Chancellor, Sir. I suggest we endorse the suggestion made by Professor Garba that a panel be set up to investigate the matter.

PROF. LAMONE LAMANG: As a matter of procedure, the arrested students must first be served with letters of rustication from the University and a directive to make themselves available before the panel for investigation. I so suggest Mr. Vice-Chancellor Sir.

VICE-CHANCELLOR: Well then, registrar serve them with the said letter immediately while we go ahead to constitute the panel. Do I speak for the Senate?

SENATE: *(In unison)* Approoooved! Approooved! Approooved!

PROF. AMINA GARBA: The Vice-Chancellor may wish to appoint the Chairman and Secretary of the panel while we suggest its members and draw up the terms of reference, as a matter of procedure, Mr. Vice-Chancellor Sir.

VICE-CHANCELLOR: I appoint Prof. Salawu Jegede of the Faculty of Law as Chairman, and Mr. Paul Jasni, the Director Security Services as secretary.

SENATE: Approoooved! Approooved! Approoooved!

PROF. HAMASEYO JAURO: *(One of the few elderly professors left in the senate. He has been silent all through until now).* My dear Senators! "Approved" is not the only response to whatever the V.C. has said. Can't you do more than shouting in monotone?

PROF. WAWA: Our Professor Emeritus, could you suggest a more pleasing word, term, phrase or sentence we can use to express our support and loyalty to our Lord, the Vice-Chancellor?

PROF. HAMASEYO JAURO: Good! Prof. Wawa, our Orator and our Ombudsman, you have just said it. The Vice-Chancellor is our Lord, then address him so for a change.

REGISTRAR: How if I may ask Sir, so that we can put it on record as part of the lexicon of the Senate of our great University?

PROF. HAMASEYO JAURO: 'As it pleases your lordship' carries more prestige than just shouting "Approved"

VICE-CHANCELLOR: I will take that as a compliment, coming from our Professor Emeritus in Lexicology. Isn't it Sir?

PROF. HAMASEYO JAURO: As it pleases your Lordship.

VICE-CHANCELLOR: University Orator, please popularize the phrase.

PROF. WAWA: As it pleases your Lordship.

VICE-CHANCELLOR: Director Senate please take note.

DIRECTOR SENATE: As it pleases your Lordship.

VICE-CHANCELLOR: The panel must submit its report within two days. Registrar, remember what I said: do not serve the Treasurer any suspension letter, she is innocent, I insist.

REGISTRAR: As it pleases your Lordship

SENATORS: (*Chant in chorus*) As it pleases your Lordship, As it pleases your Lordship, As it pleases your Lordship.

BLACK OUT

MOVEMENT NINE

Panel's first sitting. Students are called in one after the other.

FIRST STUDENT: (*Enters boisterously, faces the audience and billows*) Greeeeeeat Nigerian Students!

AUDIENCE: GREAT!

FIRST STUDENT: Greeeeeeat Nigerian Students!

AUDIENCE: GREAT!

FIRST STUDENT: Greeeeeeat Nigerian Students!

AUDIENCE: GREAT!

He takes a seat pointed to him by the panel's secretary. He sits down facing the panellists defiantly.

PANEL'S SECRETARY: What is your full name?

FIRST STUDENT: My full name is Sanusi Mohammed

PANEL'S SECRETARY: Which department and what year?

FIRST STUDENT: Department of English, final year!

PANEL'S SECRETARY: Do you know why you are here before the panel?

FIRST STUDENT: Yes I do. I got a letter from the panel asking me to appear before it to answer questions on the disturbance that took place two nights ago.

PANEL'S CHAIRMAN: What were you doing at the V.C.'s Guest House that night when the security men apprehended you?

FIRST STUDENT: I was not at the Guest House that night, I was going to the class to read when the security men accosted me and dragged me to the duty room.

PANEL'S CHAIRMAN: What do you know about the students' protest that night, who were the masterminds of the crisis?

FIRST STUDENT: The protest was necessitated by the Kangaroo mentality of the Vice-Chancellor, especially the suppression of our rights as students in the University, our right to conduct elections and form a Student Union Government of our own and be accountable to ourselves.

PANEL'S CHAIRMAN: Do you subscribe to that allegation then?

FIRST STUDENT: Surely, I do.

PROF. AMINA GARBA: How come then that you are not part of the protest with all the strong sentiments that you have against the Vice-Chancellor.

FIRST STUDENT: I don't believe in protest, I believe in due process.

PROF. LAMONE LAMANG: What suggestion do you have for the panel?

FIRST STUDENT: I don't have any suggestion, I have an advice: Be on the right side of History!

PANEL'S CHAIRMAN: If there are no further questions from members, I think the student can leave.

Next student enters, he remains standing briefly before the Panel Secretary points to him a seat. He does not seat immediately not until he gives the audience his own salutation with clenched fist thrusting up into space.

SECOND STUDENT: *Aluta Continua!*

AUDIENCE: *Victoria Acerta!*

SECOND STUDENT: *Aluta Continua!*

AUDIENCE: *Victoria Acerta!*

PANEL'S CHAIRMAN: (*Shouts at him*) Enough of this nonsense. This is the Senate Chamber not the Students Centre.

PANEL'S SECRETARY: What is your full name?

SECOND STUDENT: My full name is Chukwude Igwe

PANEL'S SECRETARY: Which department and what year?

SECOND STUDENT: Department of Human Anatomy, Final Year student.

PANEL'S SECRETARY: You went to the Vice-Chancellor's house at night with the intention to kill him, what do you need his corpse for? Don't you have enough cadavers in your Laboratory for practicals?

SECOND STUDENT: You're entitled to your opinion Sir, but the fact is that as students we hold our lecturers and leaders in high esteem, and as a student of Human Anatomy I value life as something sacred.

DR. KIMARAM TIWE: Answer the chairman's question please, do not lecture us about morality here.

SECOND STUDENT: With all due respect Sir, the chairman only expressed an opinion in an interrogative tone, otherwise called rhetorical question. It deserves no answer.

PANEL'S CHAIRMAN: Are you a student of English or Human Anatomy?

SECOND STUDENT: We learn from each other sir, that's why students are mixed in their rooms and we have Students Centre to interact meaningfully among us.

PROF. HAMASEYO JAURO: You are right. The Students Centre is like the Senate Chamber. They bear the same initials, SC. I'm happy to hear that in your own SC you debate issues intelligibly.

SECOND STUDENT: Thank you sir.

DR. KIMARAM TIWE: If you were not at the V.C.'s house to kill him, what then were you doing there with clubs, sticks and all sorts of crude weapons?

SECOND STUDENT: We went there unarmed to register our grievances and rescue one of us, a female student, held hostage at the V.C.'s Guest House.

DR. KIMARAM TIWE: Did she go there by force or by choice?

SECOND STUDENT: Either way, Sir is wrong. The University is a grove of academe not decademe.

PANEL'S CHAIRMAN: Thank you, you have said enough, you can leave now.

(Third student enters, evidently popular among her fellow students. As she cat walks to the panel the audience hail her with the chant: Zaki! Zaki! Zaki! She seats cross legged with a poise)

PROF. HAMASEYO JAURO: *(Snaps at her)* Seat properly like a well brought up girl. This is the Senate Chamber not the Guest House *(Student brings down her leg and adjusts her position but keeps a squint gaze at them).*

PANEL's SECRETARY: Tell us your full name, Department and year of study.

THIRD STUDENT: My full name is Zakinatu Joji from the Department of Education, I'm a final year English/Education student.

PANEL's CHAIRMAN: I observed that your fellow students hail you as Zaki, a male lion. I thought you should be hailed as *Zakanya*, a female lion, that is if you are a lion at all.

THIRD STUDENT: The word is "Zaky" a slang for Zakinatu, not "Zaki", I am not an animal, Sir.

PROF. WAWA: Yet you behave like an animal, stumping into the V.C.'s Guest House destroying property, searching for the V.C. to devour.

THIRD STUDENT: On the contrary Sir, I'm the one being searched for, lured to the Guest House to be devoured. I take exception to your use of language, sir. Learned men use courteous words on ladies.

PANEL's CHAIRMAN: (*Dr. Faruk, sitting next to the chairman, whispers something into the chairman's ears*) Do you mean Words like pornocracy? Pornography? "Pornetics"? Words reserved exclusively for women and female students like you, What do you say?

THIRD STUDENT: You want the answer, practical or written, Sir?

DR. KABIRU FARUK: Mr. Chairman Sir, Ms. Zakinatu appears to know too much, I think we can allow her to go and prepare a written report to zhe panel.

PANEL's SECRETARY: I agree with Dr Faruk. In view of the fact that the Chairman and some of us have another important meeting to attend, I suggest that we ask the remaining students as well to submit written reports to the panel within the next two hours. We can then deliberate through E-Communication on the investigation and bring the findings and recommendations to our next sitting for adoption.

PROF. AMINA GARBA: I concur, Mr Chairman

PROF. LAMONE LAMANG: I support Mr Chairman

DR. KIMARAM TIWE: Approved

PANEL's CHAIRMAN: Would someone then move the motion for adjournment?

PROF. WAWA: I move the motion of adjournment.

DR. KIMARAM TIWE: I support the motion.

PANEL'S CHAIRMAN: Meeting adjourned.

BLACK OUT

MOVEMENT TEN

(At the resumed sitting of the committee later that day. Members have finished deliberation and the Secretary is half way reading the committees' findings and recommendations)

PANEL'S SECRETARY: SECTION B: RECOMMENDATIONS.

1. The Students Union Government be dissolved and a new caretaker committee be set up to run the affairs of the Union.

2. Those apprehended at the premises of the Guest House be rusticated from the campus and debar them from Students Union activities for the rest of their life as students in the University.

3. The students should henceforth be allowed to elect their leaders instead of hand-picking them by the University Authorities.

4. The Treasurer, Miss Zakinatu Joji, be adequately compensated for the humiliation she suffered in the hands of her fellow students.

5. As part of the compensation, Miss Zakinatu Joji be appointed as Chairman of the Care-Taker-Government of the Students Union for continuity and accountability.

PROF. DANLADI USMAN: Continuity of what? Continuity of her promiscuity or the dubiety of her accountability as Treasurer of the Student Union Government? Mr. Secretary, where in the minutes of our deliberations was such a senseless recommendation made, is this the way you take minutes of meetings in the Administration? This is a committee headed by a Professor and dominated by senior academics, not a meeting of registry staff chaired by a Deputy Registrar. Here, there must be no prevarications with ideas, no equivocation with words, no manipulation of facts for self-gratification, as you are wont to do in the administration.

MRS RABI MAIRABO: Prof. Usman, as a Deputy Registrar of this great University I must caution you against making sweeping statements denigrating the office of the registrar and the diligence of its staff. Minutes of the last meeting were read, adopted and matters arising were discussed by all of us, how can you accuse the Secretary of distortion. Registry staff are well trained and certified administrators.

PROF. DANLADI USMAN: Who trained you and where? We trained you here as Lecturers in the Management Sciences.. The Secretary was actually my student of Public Administration, I did not teach him how to prevaricate with facts and distort unanimous decisions.

PANEL's SECRETARY: With all due respect Sir, you taught me virtually nothing. You were too busy chasing money as visiting Lecturer in nearly all the Universities of the North, that you took your primary responsibility here for granted and short changing your students. Were it not for the magnanimity of the Administration, which you are now disparaging, you will not only be demoted but be thrown out as unproductive and a liability to the University.

PANEL'S CHAIRMAN: Ladies and Gentlemen, it seems we are derailing from our course. Prof. Usman was only making an observation, all we need to do is to go back to the minutes to authenticate the recommendations.

MRS. RABI MAIRABO: Mr. Chairman Sir, minutes don't have to be explicit, atimes facts are implied not stated.

DR. KIMARAM TIWE: Who taught you that Mrs. Mairabo, I guess Prof Usman did.

MRS RABI MAIRABO: It is not only in the Management Sciences we learn Public Administration, the Department of English is in fact more useful to us than the Management Sciences. They teach public Administrators how to write official correspondences, how to take notes at meetings and how to write good minutes and recommendations without distortions.

DR. KIMARAM TIWE: It must be through e-Teaching where you can score 'A' grade in composition writing without putting pen to paper.

PROF. DANLADI USMAN: Perhaps that explains why the Secretary will take minutes of meeting and report what is not said in the meeting. That is E-Learning, which means learning to forget.

MRS. RABI MAIRABO: The E-plague is all over, we also have E-Professors, E- for Economic not Electronic this time.

PANEL'S CHAIRMAN: My Deputy Registrar what type of Professors are these, not all Professors studied Economics, anyway.

MRS. RABI MAIRABO: Yes, not all Professors Mr. Chairman, at least you are not one, and maybe Professor Usman too is not among them. But we know of many who became Professors without putting pen to paper. They publish through E-publication using economic power. All they do is pay money to the brilliant but pauperised lecturers among them to write brilliant papers and simply add their names as co-authors; putting the sponsor's name first of course.

DR. KIMARAM TIWE: Even if it were to be true, at least somebody did some writing for which somebody was promoted. It is different from being promoted on the basis of how many years you merely sat in the office drinking tea and watching UEFA on T.V. without writing anything to expand the frontiers of knowledge.

HAJIYA KUBURATU TAHIR: DR. Tiwe you need to know that not every lecturer in the University is an academic material, some of you actually have no business being in the lecture hall, the laboratory, or the library. The fact that such lecturers exist in the system and can rise to the level of a professor without writing, or at best by plagiarizing other people's work, including postgraduate student's works, makes a great ridicule of the University as a place of learning and scholarship.

DR. KIMARAM TIWE: Hajiya Tahir, but these supposedly numskull academics are the ones that taught you as a product of this university. Are you saying then that you are numbskull as well? That your degree is fake and therefore you are fake?

HAJIYA KUBURATU TAHIR: I'm not saying that there are no good lecturers in the university, there are a few of you actually. I relied on those very few among you and on my personal efforts at the internet to acquire my knowledge for which I got a well-deserved degree certificate.

PANEL'S CHAIRMAN: We are not here to debate on the qualities of academic staff and the relevance of non-academic staff in the university, please let's come back to the substantive matter before us. Professor Danladi what is your take on Zakinatu from the testimonies?

PROF. DANLADI USMAN: Investigation has shown that Zakinatu was arrested right inside the bedroom while other students were arrested outside trying to force themselves into the Guest House. Therefore, Zakinatu was actually inside the Guest House before the protesting students arrived.

PROF. WAWA: What are you insinuating? What are you suggesting she went there for?

PROF. DANLADI USMAN: Maybe we should invite the Vice-Chancellor for clarification on that Prof. Wawa, unless you can do so being his Ombudsman.

DR. KIMARAM TIWE: Actually, one of the students in his testimony alluded to an amorous relationship between Zakinatu and the vice-Chancellor. That they stormed the Guest House not to loot but to humiliate her, knowing very well she was hibernating inside instead of being with them at the rally.

PANEL's CHAIRMAN: I think Zakinatu's case has generated enough interest to this panel, I therefore wish to bring the matter to an end by appointing Dr. Kimaram Tiwe, Mrs. Rabi Mairabo and the Secretary to look at the report once again and come up with a clean copy tomorrow for signing by members. However, we must not forget that Zakinatu's name must not appear in the report, that she is innocent, that it was all a matter of coincidence that she was caught, that this is an executive order by the Vice-chancellor, our Lord.

PANEL's SECRETARY: As his Lordship pleases.

MEMBERS: (*In unison*) Approoooved.

BLACK OUT

MOVEMENT ELEVEN

A congress meeting of the local branch of the Academic Staff Union of Universities (ASUU) is underway in the University. The branch Chairman rises up to address members after the Secretary has welcomed everybody and read out the agenda of the meeting..

ASUU CHAIRMAN: Dear colleagues, ladies and gentlemen. On behalf of our National President, I welcome you back from the long and arduous strike. I must commend the doggedness and stoicism with which you stood up to the insouciance and the attendant highhandedness of the Federal Government towards our legitimate demands and patriotic struggle. Accordingly, I thank the leadership of our great University, especially the Vice-Chancellor, for the support and understanding shown to us during the long strike. This is the first time University administration stood solidly behind its striking lecturers in the history of our union.

DR. MADU BALAMI: *(interjects angrily)* Arrant nonsense, bullshit! The Vice Chancellor supported the strike like all other Vice Chancellors across the Nigerian Universities because of their selfish interest. They thought that ASUU was going on strike to fight against the inclusion of the Federal Universities in Treasury Single Account. They are irked by it because it the plugged the leakages through which they steal University money and stifle the system.

ASUU SECRETARY: Dr Balami you are out of order, allow the Chairman to finish his address, please.

DR. MADU BALAMI: I'm sorry sir for interjecting. The Chairman actually started on a wrong footing (sits down)

ASUU CHAIRMAN: As I was saying before I was rudely interrupted...

DR. MADU BALAMI: *(rises up again in protest)* I did not interrupt you; I merely interjected to call you to order...

ASUU SECRETARY: Dr Balami, please allow this meeting to take up properly.

ASUU CHAIRMAN: I need the protection of the congress to make my points, please.

PROF. TEMBO MOKOLKOLIRE: Young man please allow the chairman to finish what he wants to say, there will be enough time to respond to him.

ASUU CHAIRMAN: Thank you sir, I now feel protected to continue. Indeed we need to be excluded from the Treasury Single Account for financial autonomy and self-accounting, just as we also need to own and operate our pension scheme.

You must have read in our latest bulletin, details of the agreement signed by our Union and the Federal Government, and the breakdown of the money released so far to each University in the country. I'm pleased to reiterate that, our University has already received its share of ₦2b as revitalization fund.

May I also inform you that, in our meeting with the Vice-Chancellor yesterday on the expenditure profile of the revitalization fund, we were adequately briefed on the projects and activities earmarked for execution. These include construction of extensive drainage system, upgrading of roads on the campus, construction of security fences, provision of solar panels for the generation of light at strategic areas and buildings in the University, among other laudable projects. The floor is now open for discussion on this matter and other issues. Thank you.

DR. DALLA DALLA: Mr Chairman, members of congress. My name is Dr. Dalla Dalla of the Department of Veterinary Medicine, where doctors treat and eat their patients, but I'm not here to eat you anyway. (*Laughter from members*) Mr. Chairman Sir, from your explanation it is obvious that the money released to the university is all for infrastructural development and upgrade of administrative facilities. Is that what we went on five months strike for? What about our welfare which was the rallying point of the strike? What is happening to our Earned Academic Allowance which was the number one issue on our list of demands? What is happening to our demand for increased funding for research and publication which is frustrating promotions in the University? You talked about excluding the University from the TSA and

Pension scheme, are these part of our priorities? Who is afraid of TSA but the kleptomaniacs in the administration? We have a history of squandermania and kleptocracy in this University which we as members of ASUU could not checkmate because of our complacency and sometimes complicity in the crimes.

ASUU CHAIRMAN: *(Interjects)* Dr. Dalla Dalla you are digressing, please address the cogent issues and be brief.

DR. DALLA DALLA: Mr. Chairman, I don't know of any cogent issue more than these. I think I have made my point, thank you.

(More hands come up from members wanting to contribute to the deliberations. The chairman recognizes one of them.)

MR HARUNA DAUDA: Thank you Mr. Chairman. My name is *Farmacist* Haruna Dauda from the department of Crop Science, we produce what we eat and feed others as well. Therefore, talking about Earned Academic Allowance, nobody earns it better than us. We teach and produce not only self-employed graduates but also food to feed the nation.

ASUU CHAIRMAN: Sorry Mr. Farmer. Please get to the point straight and be brief.

MR HARUNA DAUDA: Thank you Mr. Chairman, I will try to be brief and straight to the point. Mr. Chairman Sir, ASUU should stop behaving like the Nigerian lawyers who will file a fifty count charge in court just to gamble for a ruling on one or two.

BARR. YUSUF MUSA: (*Interjects*) Objection my lord, sorry I mean my Chairman. The young farmer is sowing his seeds beyond the borders of his farmland. He should draw his examples and precedence from his crops not from the courts where he is a layman.

CONGRESS: (*Shouting excitedly*) Objection overruled! Objection Overruled!

ASUU SECRETARY: Order! Congress Order! Please. (*Silence prevails as Mr. Haruna remains standing waiting to continue*).

ASUU CHAIRMAN: Objection sustained, Farmer Haruna please be brief and direct. You have just a minute to conclude.

MR HARUNA DAUDA: As I was saying before I my learned colleague interrupted...

BARR YUSUF MUSA: (*Interjects again*) Objection! My lord...

ASUU CHAIRMAN: Objection over ruled! Please this is ASUU congress meeting not a moot court for the display of sophistry. Mr Dauda you have thirty seconds.

MR HARUNA DAUDA: Mr. Chairman, thank you for the protection. Permit me to educate the assumedly learned barrister that farmers are not laymen anywhere. As farmers our products are all over the place, you can find food even in the streets. Tell me my

Lord Barrister, where in the streets can one find justice?

BARRISTER YUSUF MUSA: Justice is not a destitute you can find in the streets; it has integrity, dignity, and self-respect. If you search with honest eyes you will see justice even in the dark; if you have pure heart you will enjoy justice even in the grave: if you come with clean hands you will be given justice even without asking for it. Its justice and equity that brought us together here otherwise, my dear farmer, you belong to the farm.

DR. MADU BALAMI: Mr. Chairman sir, may I remind these verbal acrobats that this is a meeting of ASUU not arse holes, excuse my language please. What is the difference? The farmer has his *farm*, the lawyer also has his *firm*; it's all a matter of spelling. As for the law, you only need to add the letter 'n' and you are a piece of land in the hands of the farmer.

ASUU CHAIRMAN: No more of these banter please, I think we have had enough of the comic relief for a flip. Professor Mokolkolire your mouth has ideas.

PROF. TEMBO MOKOLKOLIRE: (*Rises with deliberate slowness after being recognized by the Chairman to speak*) Dear Congress men and women, our problem as an academic union is lack of unity of purpose. This has made us become mere puns in the hands of the Federal Government and University authorities. Most times we go on a nation-wide strike to demand for things that are not relevant to our circumstances. We ignore our welfare, which is indispensable to our productivity, and pursue peripheral issues. Why should it be ASUU that must go on strike to demand for increased funding to the Universities instead of University administrators? How much control do we have over the way funds are utilized in our University? We went on five months strike, we suffered all humiliations, while other people in the system just sat idle in their cosy offices waiting for us to attract funds for them to squander. Tell me how did funds meant for the improvement of academic facilities go into buying luxury cars for Principal officers, funding of circus conferences for non-academic staff and construction of luxury suites and Guest houses in Abuja for the indulgence of the principal officers of the University, and that includes the officers of our Union of course? How would it have been if there monies were meant for our personal welfare? We will not only be motivated to perform optimally but we would have become more creative and active to conduct productive researches with far less grants

At this point, Zakinatu and five other female students breezed into the hall pushing trolleys full of snacks and drinks. She supervises the girls as they serve the congress but she also listens with keen ears to what is being said as the meeting continues)

ASUU CHAIRMAN: Prof. Mokolkolire, I share with you your sentiments. But you must also acknowledge the fact that the luxury suites cater for all staff of the University who enjoy 10% discount at the hotel whenever we are in Abuja. Besides, the suites are major revenue earners and avenues for Academic tourism for the University being in a strategic city of the country. You must not forget too that a substantial part of the money went into funding researches by academic staff, is that not an aspect of staff welfare?

PROF. TEMBO MOKOLKOLIRE: Mr Chairman you are entitled to your opinion about our welfare, but you must know on which side to stand. We are talking of a whopping amount of 2 billion naira released to our University! And in addition do you know how much our sixty room luxury suites in Abuja generate as revenue each day? Mr. Chairman, Sir, do not underrate our intelligence. Thank you.

DR. MADU BALAMI: (*Puts up his hand*) Point of correction Mr. Chairman.

ASUU CHAIRMAN: Yes Dr. Balami, what is it?

DR. MADU BALAMI: The number of accessible rooms to guests at the University Suites is just thirty not the entire sixty. The remaining rooms have been shared among the principal officers and members of the Vice-Chancellor's "chicken cabinet". The daily revenue realized from the remaining rooms I guess go into paying the staff and stuffing the kitchen to feed their girlfriends who are permanently kept in those rooms.

At this point, Zakinatu comes around with drinks and as she passes by, she trips on the steps and her handbag falls right in front of Dr. Balami. A key falls out of the bag with the name of the University suites on the key holder. Dr. Balami quickly picks up the key before she could do so.

DR. MADU BALAMI: Mr. Chairman before you disagree with me on the misuse of the University facilities here is an evidence (*Shows up the key*) This is a key to one of the executive rooms of the University Suites. It fell out from the handbag of this seductive young lady who is apparently also an ad-hoc staff of ASUU Secretariat. (*Turns to Zakinatu*) Young lady, are you also a staff of the University Suites or one of the regular guests of the place?

ZAKINATU JOJI: Objection, my love...Sorry I mean...Sir. I'm the Treasurer of the S.U.G. and just as the ASUU executive members and Principal offices of the University are entitled to personalized rooms in our Abuja Suites, S.U.G executives also enjoy the same privilege. As you can see we are here to serve you during your meeting, this is how we also serve principal officers of the University. I'm always on the flight with the Chief Executive whenever he travels to Abuja to serve him there. This is the key to the Executive room which is entrusted to me.

DR. MADU BALAMI: Young lady, thank you for being here to serve your lecturers with drinks and snacks during meeting, even though you ought not do that. But would you tell us how you serve the Chief Executive at the Abuja Suites? Do you serve him at the reception, at the restaurant or as room service? Are you truly a student?

PROF. TEMBO MOKOLKOLIRE: Dear colleagues, there appears to be a serious moral issue in what the young lady has just divulged here, and the very serious insinuations contained in Dr. Balami's question. Mr. Chairman Sir, what do you know about this case, and is it a mere coincidence or a conspiracy that she is here to serve us in our meeting? I hope we don't have other spies among us here.

ZAKINATU JOJ: I'm not a spy Prof., I'm a student please.

PROF. TEMBO MOKOLKOLIRE: All lizards lay flat on their stomach, no one can tell which one has stomach pain by merely looking at them.

ASUU CHAIRMAN: Well, I know that this young lady is always on the plane whenever the Chief Executive is traveling to Abuja. Until now, I thought she was the Chief Protocol Officer of the University who takes Personal care of the Chief executive. I contacted her to assist our secretariat with entertainment in this meeting not knowing that she is actually a student. Young lady, thank you for your services, I think you can leave with your group now.

(*Zakinatu leaves the hall reluctantly*)

DR. DALLA DALLA: This deceptive female student has caused us a lot of distraction, I suspect she was sent here to spy on us. But it also says a lot about the moral integrity of the Vice-Chancellor.

ASUU CHAIRMAN: Dr. Dalla Dalla, it seems you are also creating more distractions. What the Vice Chancellor does with beautiful female students should not bother us here. Being a young man who has only now came to limelight, it will be difficult to tame his desires to sow the wild oats.

DR. DALLA DALLA: Mr. Chairman, I'm disappointed with your opinion on this matter, but let us not be distracted any further. What is the next item on the agenda; I think it is the issue of nepotism and abuse of due process in employment in the University.

ASUU SECRETARY: Mr. Chairman, dear colleagues, the remaining issues of staff employment, nepotism, misuse of IGR and issuance of bogus contracts are too weighty to be discussed within the short time left before it is Zuhr. I therefore suggest we adjourn the meeting to 2pm for members to go for lunch and observe the afternoon prayer. I so move, Mr. Chairman.

PROF. TEMBO MOKOLKOLIRE: I second the motion moved by the secretary for adjournment till 2pm.

BLACK OUT

MOVEMENT TWELVE

At the Vice Chancellor's Guest house, Zakinatu is in the middle of a heated argument with the Vice Chancellor.

V.C.: Zakinatu I must say that you are very lucky to have this deal. Now we can lay the matter to rest.

ZAKINATU JOJI: Objection my love! I'm not a toy you can play with. I need a concrete proposal, a definite commitment or else...

V.C.: Or else what?

ZAKINATU JOJI: Or else we go down the drain together!!

V.C.: You are mischievous (*sounds like Miss Chievous*)

ZAKINATU JOJI: Sorry, I'm not Miss Chievous, that must be one of your numerous girlfriends. I'm Miss Joji and soon to be Mrs Yours.

V.C.: I mean you're full of mischief, don't misunderstand me.

ZAKINATU JOJI: Then mind your pronunciation, and as for mischief you have not seen anything yet.

V.C.: Tell me what exactly you want and stop being a pain in the neck. I've explained everything to you, I've given you the assurance that you will come out clean in the matter. What further assurance do you want?

ZAKINATU JOJI: The problem is not about the matter. I can handle the matter myself and come out clean without your help. The so-called Senate Disciplinary

Committee is unwisely composed of mainly men, and you know very well my power of seduction over men.

V.C.: Your power of seduction notwithstanding, I had to give an executive directive to the committee to exculpate you of all accusations. I virtually dictated to the committee's secretary the recommendations of the report that will not only exonerate you but also compensate you for the embarrassments. What else do you want?

ZAKINATU JOJI: Unfortunately your directives did not work. There are professors on the committee who are older than you that you cannot dictate to them. I had to put my power of seduction to proper use and blindfold them of my alleged crime.

V.C.: Madam Seduction, what exactly do you want me to do now? State your price, make your demands; I am getting rather sick and tired of this Ostrich mentality of yours.

ZAKINATU JOJI: Sick and tired indeed! You have seen beneath the plumage of the Ostrich now you have the shameless boldness to say that its ugly flesh is sickening to your taste. Well you have savoured the flesh and now there is a rapture- I'm pregnant.

V.C.: (*Gives out a loud and long derisive laughter*) Is blackmail also an act of seduction? I thought you will use the power of entreaty rather than intimidation to sustain the covetousness of your admirers.

ZAKINATU JOJI: I'm neither short of admirers nor running out of time for a settled relationship. It's one thing to be a sybarite and quite another to be a libertine. You are the only man I know intimately, and obviously you are the only one I'm associated with publicly. At least, your office maid, my roommates, the stewards and the house keeper here in the Guest House can testify to our close relationship.

V.C.: And who will testify to the cause of the rapture?

ZAKINATU JOJI: My dear Vice Chancellor Sir, I may be just a student to the best of your knowledge, and if you are indulgent enough you may also know me as a good time friend. Well for your information, I'm also a police detective from the DSS posted here along with my other colleagues. Look here if you must know (*points to her chest*) the pendant of my necklace is a high definition omniscient camera. If you were careful you would have noticed that each time we were in the bedroom I hung it strategically facing the bed. Does that answer your question about witness to the cause?

Now completely flummoxed the V.C. sinks himself in the sofa, staring blankly at space away from her. a knock on the door, Zakinatuu quickly disappears through the back door. Enter ASUU Chairman.

ASUU CHAIRMAN: Good afternoon Sir, you look pensive, I'm sure Zakinatu has furnished you with the tape recording of the meeting.

V.C.: Not yet, any complications?

ASUU CHAIRMAN: A lot of revelations about the misuse of funds and abuse of University facilities especially the University hotel. Zakinatu too did not help matters with her carelessness in handling the hotel room key in her possession. She let it fall out of her handbag right in front of Dr. Balami just as he was making damaging revelations about the University hotel. I invited Zakinatu to spy on some of the lecturers and record their utterances for your consumption but she has failed us this time. However Barrister Yusuf and self-styled **Farmacist** Haruna acted very well the clowns we asked them to be. The banters they engaged in as contributions to the debate in the congress helped in diverting attention and causing delay in reaching a decision. Indeed the meeting ended inconclusively.

V.C.: That's good, I can now release Barrister Yusuf's promotion to Professorship with a retrospective effect. I will also announce the appointment of our Farmer as the new university farm director and give him enough slush funds to run the place. However, I must tell you that we are in a big trouble with Zakinatu. She is spying for us and on us too. She is a double agent and has all the secrets of the University with her.

ASUU CHAIRMAN: We also have enough of her secrets to silence her with. Remember that she was admitted with forged result and she never passed most of her courses.

V.C.:   She was never a student in the first place. She was planted on the University by the DSS and she is not the only one spying on us. We need to know who the others are, and they may even be posing as staff among us. We must negotiate with them.

ASUU CHAIRMAN: Mr. Vice-Chancellor Sir, as we say in Hausa, *'biri yayi kama da mutum'* I find Prof. Wawa's loyalty too extreme to be genuine. He must be one of them. He is yet to speak at the ASUU congress this morning but I'm sure he will say something when the meeting resumes later at 2pm.

V.C.:   My Chairman, in the light of this development we must suspend the planned disbursement of the research funds and divert the money to damage control measures. I hope your members are yet to know about the money.

ASUU CHAIRMAN: I was to use that as a bait to placate the congress when we resume later in the day, but now it must be a sacred secret. However, members of the executive must get their 10% share of the funds which translates to 10million naira for each member. In fact I was virtually alone in shielding the V.C. at the meeting this morning, my executive members were complicitly silent throughout the meeting. They must get their alert before 2pm today lest we risk their loyalty.

V.C.:   We can't afford further damages at this point. I will instruct the bursar to post the money to their accounts before the meeting.

ASUU PRESIDENT: Thanks Sir. I must rush for the afternoon prayer, the meeting resumes at exactly 2pm.

BLACK OUT

MOVEMENT THIRTEEN

Zakinatu on stage addressing the audience. This time she appears rather sober, decorous, devoid of any derring-do.

ZAKINATU JOJI: Every job has its risks. I'm a Detective Police Officer under the cover of student. I hold a Bachelor of law degree from the University of Maiduguri, and a Master's degree in Fraud Detection and Prevention in Public Institutions from Ahmadu Bello University Zaria. Currently I'm a senior Investigator in the operations department of the Economic and Financial Crime Commission (EFCC) on a special assignment here in the University. But as I have said, the job has its jeopardy.

It is not easy for me playing the role of a seductive detective. Seduction is a very effective technique of crime detection, especially financial and moral crimes. The law of seduction says "seduce or be seduced". I suffered a lot trying to apply the law. I faced temptations and blackmail from both staff and students, I suffered harassment and embarrassment from female staff who keep lustful eyes on their male counterparts, I experienced real beating from wives of lecturers for my derring-dos with their spouses. But I must confess that my worst trials and tribulations in the act of seduction came from this vibrant, ebullient, vivacious, charismatic, sexually active and attractive young man, your Vice-Chancellor.

But the trials were worth the results. Were it not for my closeness with the Vice-Chancellor, I wouldn't have discovered how deep in decadence this place is. I have discovered that the University is a centre of excellence not in any particular field of learning and scholarship, but in megalomania, kleptocracy and debauchery. But I did not do this alone, I have my assistants from the Force Headquarters. Detective Hauwa Ibrahim known to you in the romantic poetry class as Pink Lady is very exceptional in emotional seduction. (*Enter pink lady walking with panache. Zakinatu pauses with a poise*)

PINK LADY: Yes, my name is Hauwa Ibrahim, the Pink Lady. I must say that some lecturers really suffer a lot of emotional harassment and sexual blackmail from some female students in this University. We are now better informed than the one-sided stories we hear about lecturers sexually harassing female students. Actually, female students, especially the academically weak but physically beautiful ones like me, are the ones harassing the male lecturers and blackmailing female lecturers. Of course some lecturers do harass female students as was done to Miss Lamila by the ophthalmologist at the teaching hospital. I'm sure there are some among you too who have had similar experiences but you chose to remain silent for fear of victimisation.

ZAKINATU JOJI: Indeed we must commend you for your patience in the face of brazen oppression. However, in as much as we commend you for the maturity we strongly condemn your docility towards the suppression of your rights and financial exploitation. I served as Treasurer of the Students Union Government, supposedly your own government. Do you know how much you are worth financially? Your Union dues amounts to over ₦50,000,000! Do you know how the money is spent, for who and by who? Are your Union leaders accountable to you? How can they when they are not elected by you but hoisted on you by the University authority. Anyway, I don't blame you, when the apparently independent and seemingly enlightened unions such as ASUU and SANU are themselves too docile to demand accountability from the University authority on the use of its internally generated revenue and other sundry incomes from government. My detective colleague, the so-called Professor Wawa has all the records of the financial scam in the University. (*Enter Professor Wawa, light dims on Zakinatu to shine on him*)

PROF. WAWA: Yes I'm Prof. Wawa, the ear, mouth and eyes of the Vice Chancellor, and by the grace of his Royal Lordship. I'm also the Ombudsman of the Senate and Orator of the University. But I must now confess to you that I don't have even a Diploma qualification. I joined the Nigeria Police with my Grade II certificate and rose through the ranks to become a police

Inspector. I joined the University with fake credentials as a PhD holder. The administration may have suspected but turned its eyes the other way. My colleagues in the department were also too busy chasing promotional publications and visiting other Universities for monetary gain that they did not have time to care about the academic qualities of their colleagues.

However, I must commend the circumspection and intelligence of the students in the department who were quick to observe my academic deficiency, which their lecturers were not professional enough to detect. The alarm you raised about it nearly exposed my real identity, but this is Nigeria. Just shout "Jesus"! or scream *"Allahu Akbar"* and you will see the crowd coming out to defend you. I used religion to divide the department over the matter and I won. Today, I'm not only accepted as a qualified lecturer but also a full-fledged Professor within a space of just three years. Don't mind the academic publications, not all lecturers are rich but the poor among them are also the most brilliant. They can add your name to their papers for a token.

My clowning in the Senate and praise-singing for the Vice-Chancellor is my version of seduction. My female colleagues here used the power of emotional seduction to investigate the moral conduct of principal officers and academics in your University. I used psychological seduction to penetrate the hearts and minds of the

University leadership to uncover their financial crimes. How does the University expend its IGR? They use it to buy traditional titles, build houses for their girlfriends, embark on frivolous overseas travels, and canvass for political offices. How did the University expend the whooping two billion naira given to it by the Federal Government for the revitalization of academic facilities? The money has been turned to severance gratuity for principal officers and reward for loyalty to their academic cronies including myself. Just a while ago, I received a bank alert of ₦3m from the University for what I do not know. I guess they want me to be their ombudsman at the ASUU meeting against the Union's plan to invite the EFCC to look into the financial activities of the University.

ZAKINATU JOJI: Prof. Wawa you can now tell ASUU not to bother calling the EFCC, we are here already. The outcome of our investigation will soon be made public with action.

PINK LADY: As a woman, I can see that one of us seems to show signs of the outcome.

ZAKINATU JOJI: I said it earlier that, every job has its jeopardy!

BLACK OUT

MOVEMENT FOURTEEN

At the resumed meeting of ASUU. Members are about to take resolutions.

ASUU CHAIRMAN: Prof. Wawa, as the University Orator and Ombudsman of the senate you may want to say something before we take the resolutions Sir.

PROF. WAWA: Thank you Mr Chairman for the ALERT, I'm very much aware of my responsibility and your expectation. Certainly, we are not going to throw away the dirty water together with the baby.

DR. MADU BALAMI: (*Interrupting*) Prof Wawa please be precise, no equivocation, this is the democratic congress of ASUU not the circus caucus of the senate. What alert are you referring to and whose baby is in the dirty water?

PROF. WAWA: Dr. Balami, unfortunately you are responsible for throwing away the baby with the dirty water. If you had not exposed the content of that female student's handbag, she would have told us whose baby she was carrying.

ASUU CHAIRMAN: Prof. Wawa, I must observe that you are not acting according to the alert. Is the volume not loud enough for you or are you not what you are?

PROF. TEMBO MAKOLKOLIRE: Again! Here we go. Metaphors, similes, dramatic ironies, confusion, distractions. That's the lot of us academics. Mr Chairman Sir, members of congress, rather than waste more precious time talking in tongues saying nothing but balderdash, I suggest that we state our grievances briefly record them clearly and submit them accordingly to the Vice Chancellor as the resolutions of the Academic Staff Union of Universities (ASUU) of this branch.

DR. LARABA USMAN: Mr. Chairman, members of congress our grievances are not only with the University but also the Federal government and the leadership of ASUU as well. Therefore, rather than rush to take resolutions, I suggest we set up a committee to articulate the issues listed on the agenda and come up with recommendations for deliberation in another congress meeting to be fixed within the week.

DR. MAIRAMA ANGO: The smaller the committee the better, I suggest a membership of only three people with Prof. Mokolkolire as the head.

CONGRESS: Approved! Approved!! Approved!!!

DR. DAUDA BALAMI: For the avoidance of doubt, let me read out the full list of our grievances, some of which are not on the agenda of the meeting.

ASUU CHAIRAMAN: Dr. Balami please we must keep to the agenda as circulated for the meeting.

DR. DALLA DALLA: Mr. Chairman Sir, you are overruled on this matter. If it is the wish of the congress to add other issues to the agenda you cannot rule on that. The setting up of a committee was not on the agenda but we endorsed it because it made sense in the circumstance. Therefore, if there is need to add other issues to the agenda we must allow that.

CONGRESS: Allowed! Allowed!! Allowed!!!

PROF. WAWA: In that case even the committee may not be necessary as we can straight away state our views. However, given the fact that the attendance at this meeting is very poor we can only state our points and allow the committee to draft a resolution for ratification at the next congress meeting. The points we are going to make should be distributed to every member of ASUU to attract them to the next meeting.

DR. MAIRAMA ANGO: I think it will be more expedient if we list our grievances right away and then delegate the EXCO to present them to the Vice-Chancellor.

PROF. TEMBO MAKOLKOLIRE: Dr Ango's suggestion makes a lot of sense, I support it.

ASUU CHAIRAMAN: In that case, may I invite contributions from the congress.

Members debate their grievances while the secretary notes the resolutions. The director of the play may work out the list of grievances to reflect the existing reality of the particular University, if the play is taking place in a given University.

BLACK OUT

MOVEMENT FIFTEEN

At the headquarters of the Economic and Financial Crimes Commission (EFCC). Detective Sgt Zakinatu Joji has just finished briefing the Operations Department on her assignment to the University and hands over to the Director of Operations her written report.

DIRECTOR OPERATIONS: Thank you Sgt Joji and your team for a thorough job at the University. Your report will be forwarded to the legal department for scrutiny preparatory to prosecution. However, while I commend you for professional conduct I must express my displeasure over your gross ethical misconduct. You need not go that far to perform your duty well, there are many subtle ways you can follow to arrive at your goal. Our advice to vulnerable female detectives has always been, seduce but don't be seduced. Detective Joji, you have woefully failed in this emotional principle.

ZAKINATU JOJI: I accept full responsibility for my emotional conduct, which is certainly not in tandem with the ethical training we received in the Police. I wish I had acted otherwise, but unfortunately Sir, the power of passion is sometimes stronger than the power of seduction.

DIRECTOR OPERATIONS: Same thing too in the Police; morality is sometimes placed above professionalism. In your briefing you indicted the Vice-Chancellor of immoral conduct in addition to gross financial crimes. We are certainly taking the matter to court and you are to lead the prosecution in the trial. How then would you feel prosecuting the Vice-Chancellor for an offence that you are an accomplice to?

ZAKINATU JOJI: Sir, this is a matter of opportunity cost between expedience and exigency. The Vice-Chancellor's conduct is an act of professional irresponsibility while mine is that of professional hazard. I sacrificed my honour and integrity for a greater public interest, if I were a staff of the University I would have been rewarded for professional hazard.

DIRECTOR OPERATIONS: My dear woman, this is a matter of code of professional conduct not the solipsist niceties of the Ivory Tower. In the Police we have several ways of getting to the root of a problem without self-indulgence. The use of sexual inducement, no matter the exigency, is a grievous professional misconduct. The ethical committee of the commission has since considered your case and has recommended that you be demoted to the rank of a corporal and be redeployed to the Force Headquarters for further action.

(*Zakinatu stands up, salutes the D.O.P. with alacrity and walks out in quick march*)

BLACK OUT

MOVEMENT SIXTEEN

At the V.C.'s Guest House. He is seen sitting in a pensive mood. Zakinatu enters holding a white envelope, she drops it on his laps and sits down facing him.

VICE CHANCELLOR: What? Another invitation from the EFCC?

ZAKINATU JOJI: Open it and read, it's not an invitation but something serious.

VICE CHANCELLOR: (*Reads letter quietly*) What! You're resigning from your Job. Why?

ZAKINATU JOJI: Yes, I'm resigning from the Police. I was demoted to the rank of a Corporal when I was expecting a promotion to an Inspector.

VICE CHANCELLOR: What offence did you commit to warrant your demotion?

ZAKINATU JOJI: That I've compromised my integrity by indulging emotionally with you, and my present condition was an open evidence that I'm no longer trustworthy to continue on the job. I was then redeployed back to the Force Headquarters where I was advised to resign honourably from the Police Force.

VICE CHANCELLOR: How much does the EFCC pay you in a month? I can give you double the amount if you can

take up appointment as the Chief Security Officer of
the University.

ZAKINATU JOJI: NO! That can be risky for both of us
knowing our antecedent in the University. Besides, it is
not about now but the future in terms of job security.
You can use executive fiat to employ me against good
reason, but once you leave the office the new Vice
Chancellor can decide to terminate my contract
employment. You asked earlier if the letter was
another invitation from the EFCC?

VICE CHANCELLOR: Yes. I received earlier on a letter from
the EFCC inviting me for a routine interaction at their
Headquarters. I guess the invitation has something to
do with what you reported on your assignment here in
the University. Is it a *déjà vu* or a premonition but I
have this feeling that we are sinking together.

ZAKINATU JOJI: Actually, I'm the one sinking now and I
would rather you pull me out than for me to drag you
down with me. Let's team up.

VICE CHANCELLOR: How?

ZAKINATU JOJI: The Pregnancy!

VICE CHANCELLOR: Yes, what about it?

ZAKINATU JOJI: Let's terminate it and then there will be
no evidence of misconduct.

VICE CHANCELLOR: Then what?

ZAKINATU JOJI: Then I can appeal the judgment and return
to the Police.

VICE CHANCELLOR: Then what?

ZAKINATU JOJI: Don't forget, I still hold the four aces! There is no way the EFCC can prosecute you without my active participation. I can distort the evidences and make frivolous apologies for wrong conclusions. It may still cost me my job but I would have saved you and your principal officers from going to jail.

VICE CHANCELLOR: What a brilliant idea! I must start pulling you out of the quagmire right away by promising you marriage after the case. Meanwhile, I'm transferring to your account the sum of ₦3m to take care of the abortion and your health. As your fate in the Police is now dicey you may be asked to vacate the Police accommodation you are now occupying. As a proactive measure I'm going to purchase a four bedroom house for you soon.

ZAKINATU JOJI: What will be the status of the house, my matrimonial home or my material gain from the game?

VICE CHANCELLOR: The house is both your severance gratuity and wedding gift; it has nothing to do with your matrimonial home.

ZAKINATU JOJI: Then I would want the house to be in my home town for the comfort of my parents and siblings.

VICE CHANCELLOR: Consider it done, it's a deal.

ZAKINATU JOJI: Signed and sealed!

BLACK OUT

MOVEMENT SEVENTEEN

At the headquarters of the Economic and Financial Crimes Commission (EFCC). The Vice Chancellor and some of his principal officers are being cross examined by the director operations of the EFCC and other operatives from the Independent Corrupt Practices and allied offences (ICPC) and the Code of Conduct Bureau (CCB)

DIRECTOR OPERATIONS: Mr. Vice Chancellor sir, eminent Professors and principal officers of the Ivory Tower, we feel highly honoured to host you in this modest environment of the headquarters of the Economic and Financial Crimes Commission. Co-hosting you here with us are also operatives from the ICPC and the CCB, our sister agencies. You must bear with me that this place is nothing compared to the architectural splendour and glamour of your Senate Building.

PROF. WAWA: That may not be unconnected with the quality of minds and brains of the occupants of the Ivory Tower, Sir.

DIRECTOR OPERATIONS: Perhaps! Yes.

VICE CHANCELLOR: It is actually true. We create what we enjoy and produce what we use.

DIRECTOR OPERATIONS: Certainly Sir. Indeed you produce the entire society. That's why the University is euphemistically referred to as the *alma mater*.

PROF. WAWA: Obviously, so. That's also why we are careful not to allow the University come to any harm through irresponsible leadership or professional misconduct.

VICE CHANCELLOR: We are doing our best in spite of the meddling of the society, people don't understand how the University operates.

DIRECTOR OPERATIONS: Exactly, Sir. That is why we are always too meticulous to point accusing fingers at the denizens of the Ivory Tower. Therefore, your invitation here today is merely interactive rather than interrogative, even if it may appear to be so.

VICE CHANCELLOR: We hope so.

PROF. WAWA: Most certainly, Yes!

DIRECTOR OPERATIONS: To begin with, Our investigation reveals that in the last ten years the University has recorded tremendous infrastructural developments, including the construction of a three star hotel in the central business district of Abuja. However, virtually all the structures were funded by the Tertiary Education Trust Fund. What have you done with the internally generated revenue (IGR) of the University in those ten years, Sir?

VICE CHANCELLOR: It's not every project in the University that is executed by the TET Fund, some were funded from our internally generated revenue which includes the 3-star hotel and other guest houses, a fifty kilometre long drainage system, twenty kilometre road rehabilitation, installation of WiFi Satellite system, construction and equipping of multipurpose ICT Centres and huge sums spent on Diesel and Electricity bills. Of course, we also spend heavily on Security given our peculiar situation.

DIRECTOR OPERATIONS: That's great, Mr Vice Chancellor. I understand also that your University receives the highest monthly allocation from Federal government due to this peculiar situation. The latest was five billion naira released to you for parameter fencing of the University. Has the fencing been done and the walls are still standing?

VICE CHANCELLOR: The project is on-going, even though not the whole amount has been released to the University.

DIRECTOR OPERATIONS: How far, so far?

VICE CHANCELLOR: Is a long time I went to the site, the Director of works is in a better position to answer this question.

DIRECTOR OF WORKS: I think the best person to answer this is the Chairman of the task force on special projects who is Professor Wawa himself.

PROF. WAWA: The project has gone far, so far. But a substantial part of the walls have collapsed due to heavy rains.

DIRECTOR OPERATIONS: From our investigation we have found out that you spend ₦20m on gas and pay ₦50m as electricity bill monthly. How many factories or industries does the University have? We also learnt that with the coming in of DISCOS and TCN to take over the affairs of electricity supply, the University was plunged into darkness for months due to disagreement over the disparity in the figures found on paper and the actual amount paid to them as monthly flat rate bill. How did you resolve the disagreement?

VICE CHANCELLOR: There was no disagreement or discrepancy in figures. The operators of the new DISCO did not understand immediately that the electricity bills of the university come in bulk as payment for both electricity consumption and gas supply to the Generators.

ICPC OPERATIVE: Mr. Vice chancellor sir, in the last few years to the present there was a drastic drop in the number of academic staff due to mass exodus from your university. Does this drop reflect a corresponding drop in the salary bills from Federal treasury?

VICE CHANCELLOR: Is a complex matter, you may not understand. But let me clarify one thing...

ICPC OPERATIVE: (cuts him politely) Not to worry sir, let's look at it differently. When government introduced the Integrated Personnel Payroll System of payment for staff of all Federal Institutions, it took the university over a year to migrate to the new system, not until the government threatened you with sanction. Why were you reluctant to do that?

VICE CHANCELLOR: It took us a long time to get our balance sheet right in terms of staff strength and emolument figures.

ICPC OPERATIVE: Why did you have to embark on a massive employment of non-essential staff at the time instead of the direly needed academic staff?

VICE CHANCELLOR: I thought our invitation here was merely interactive as you said earlier but apparently it is a full interrogative session. The pattern of questioning and flow of the conversation attest to that. Nevertheless, I and my Principal Officers are already here and we are not to shy away from any question. But I must make it clear to you that we have no skeletons in the cupboards and therefore your insinuations are not only frivolous but are also based on gross misinformation and baseless speculations. I think the officers you sent to do the investigation went and got themselves involved more with the cosy side of the University life and at the end merely cooked up stories for you.

DIRECTOR OPERATIONS: I think so too, Professor Wawa what do you have to say?

PROF. WAWA: Mr. Vice Chancellor Sir, the detectives did a thorough job and I'm one of the detectives.

VICE CHANCELLOR: (*flabbergasted*) You!

PROF. WAWA: (*Gets up, walks in slow march towards the V.C. fixing a triumphant gaze at him, walks round the*

Principal Officers with the same mien and comes back to the V.C., pats him on the shoulder and keeps the hand there while he speaks) Yes! Mr. Vice Chancellor; and the figures are therefore accurate. See you in court very, very, soon.

VICE CHANCELLOR: Prof. Wawa the traitor! Let me tell you that, the courts are like the cobwebs where small flies are caught and the great break through. See you there, Mr Fake Professor.

(Professor Wawa walks away in a slow motion towards the Director Operations, waving the V.C. and his officers goodbye)

BLACK OUT

Printed in the United States
By Bookmasters